John C. Howell, a nationally respected trial lawyer, was admitted to the Florida Bar in 1955 and to the Colorado Bar in 1970. He has also been admitted to practice before all federal and state courts in those states, including the United States Supreme Court. A graduate of the University of Miami Law School, Mr. Howell has practiced extensively in corporate law. He is now a member or former member of the American Bar Association, the Federation of Insurance Counsel, the Legal Research Institute, and the American Arbitration Association. Author of a number of law review articles, Mr. Howell has also published sixteen books to date.

THE COMPLETE CITIZEN'S LAW LIBRARY

John C. Howell

THE COMPLETE LAYMAN'S GUIDE TO FORMING A CORPORATION - IN ANY STATE

Avoid personal liability, legal fees, and unnecessary expenses

A SPECTRUM BOOK

Prentice-Hall, Inc., Englewood Cliffs, New Jersey 07632

Library of Congress Cataloging in Publication Data

Howell, John Cotton (date).
  The complete layman's guide to forming a corporation—
in any state.

  (The complete citizen's law library)
  Previous ed. published as: The layman's complete guide
to forming a corporation—in any state. 1979.
  "A Spectrum Book"
  1. Corporation law—United States—Popular works.
2. Incorporation—United States—Popular works.   I. Title.   II. Series: Complete citizen's law library.
KF1414.6.H67 1981b   346.73'066   81-17880
                           347.30666   AACR2

ISBN 0-13-161406-1 {PBK.}

This publication is designed to provide accurate and authoritative information in regard to the subject matter covered. It is sold with the understanding that the publisher is not engaged in rendering legal, accounting or other professional service. If legal advice or other expert assistance is required, the services of a competent professional person should be sought.

> —From a Declaration of Principles jointly
> adopted by a Committee of the American Bar
> Association and a Committee of Publishers.

For the purposes of editorial simplification, this publication generally uses the masculine pronoun in the generic sense, to indicate *person*. The author and the publisher are fully aware that the information in this volume pertains to women as well as men, and no discrimination is implied or intended.

PRENTICE-HALL INTERNATIONAL, INC., *London*
PRENTICE-HALL OF AUSTRALIA PTY. LIMITED, *Sydney*
PRENTICE-HALL OF CANADA, LTD., *Toronto*
PRENTICE-HALL OF INDIA PRIVATE LIMITED, *New Delhi*
PRENTICE-HALL OF JAPAN, INC., *Tokyo*
PRENTICE-HALL OF SOUTHEAST ASIA PTE. LTD., *Singapore*
WHITEHALL BOOKS LIMITED, *Wellington, New Zealand*

Contents

Subscription to, Issuance of, and Payment for Stock —
De Jure and De Facto Corporations — Status and Liability
of Members

4 Corporate Existence and Franchises 57

5 The Foreign Corporation: Doing Business in
Other States 77

Appendix A: Statement of Corporate Purposes
in Articles of Incorporation 89
Appendix B: Names and Addresses of State Offices
Where New Corporation Papers Are Filed 97
Glossary of Legal Terms 99

Preface

Most large companies have corporate legal staffs with specialists in various fields to keep the company current on the massive and constantly changing laws. Inflation has driven private legal counsel out of the reach of many small business owners. It is in response to these and other problems that The Citizens Law Library was developed. Each book in the series covers areas of the law in which you can handle your own legal cases.

Forming your own corporation is one of them. You will be surprised and delighted to learn how easy it is to form your own corporation in your state. Before getting started on your own corporation, read this book carefully for a grasp of the history and background of the basic legal principles involved. Once you have a feel for corporate laws, you can follow the steps outlined in this book to legally create your corporation, organize it to start doing business, and maintain proper corporate records.

You will learn the advantages and disadvantages of incorporation compared to other forms of business entities. You will discover the dangers of organizing a "foreign" corporation (creating your corporation in another state), its excessive costs, and the realization that once you create a foreign corporation, you cannot legally do business in your own state without registering your foreign corporation there. In addition, you will have an annual state agent fee to pay to your foreign state agent.

Once you have decided to incorporate in your home state, you simply follow the step-by-step instructions outlined here to accomplish it. Most commentators claim that legal fees for having an attorney file your incorporation papers runs from $400 to $1200 or more. I do not mean to imply that these fees are excessive. Indeed, incorporation is an important step in your business career. Yet, if you learn how to do it yourself from this book, you can save a substantial amount of money. If you do need legal advice about any aspect of the transaction, you will know what questions to ask and you will have a better understanding of the answers. Furthermore, you will have the satisfaction of doing for yourself what a layman can do without an attorney.

The basic principles of the laws of corporations are summarized in this book. There is a list of the essential forms and other documents you need to complete the transaction. However, no specific legal advice is given on specific fact situations. You are cautioned to consult your attorney when specific questions are raised by the general information presented in this book.

Form Your Own Corporation is one in a series of books helping business men and women solve many legal questions they encounter daily. Our society is becoming more complex each day. The business community is inhibited and restricted by a mass of governmental rules, regulations, directives, guidelines, and laws of all kinds. Scarcely a single business act is free from constant and continuous regulation and administrative review. Against this intricate governmental and regulatory structure one thing emerges clearly. It is that private business men and women must learn how to handle legal problems without incurring staggering legal fees, and without taking too much time from productive business operations.

Introduction

The primary objectives of this book are:

1. to explore the factors to consider in determining whether you should incorporate,
2. to give you the basic procedures and laws applicable to the creation, organization, and operation of a corporation as a business entity,
3. to enable you to determine whether, where, and under what circumstances you should incorporate, and
4. to explain in step-by-step detail how you can form your corporation under the laws of your state without a lawyer.

You are not legally required to have a lawyer to form your corporation and start your own business. However, in complex corporate transactions, you may need professional advice and counsel.

Although the laws discussed cover corporations of all sizes, this book will enable you to create and organize your own corporation with a limited number of stockholders and principals. Many business owners prefer a "closed" corporation with ownership and operation kept

1

within the family or a very small group of persons.

You will need professional help in going "public"—registering with the federal and state securities agencies for public issuance of stock, and registering under Regulation A—General Exemption of the General Rules and Regulations of the Securities and Exchange Commission. You will also need advice with complicated tax problems and significant legal questions or issues.

This is a do-it-yourself book which will enable you to know what you, as a layman, can and cannot do. Although chapters 1 and 2 contain all of the facts, information and materials you will need to create and organize your own corporation, you should review carefully chapters 3 and 4 covering the legal principles and rules governing the operation and maintenance of your corporate entity. You will be able to handle the entire transaction easier after you have a better understanding of the historical background, reasons and rationale for the legal principles found in your state statutes.

1

Selection of a Business Entity

Definitions

A corporation has been defined by the United States Supreme Court as "an artificial being, invisible, intangible, and existing only in contemplation of law" (Dartmouth College v. Woodward, 4 Wheat [US] 518, 4 L ed 629). The Supreme Court of Missouri has defined it as follows:

> A corporation may be described as being an artificial being, existing only in contemplation of law; a legal entity, a fictitious person, vested by law with the capacity of taking and granting property and transacting business as an individual. It is composed of a number of individuals, authorized to act as if they were one person. The individual stockholders are the constituents or component parts through whose intelligence, judgment, and discretion the corporation acts. The affairs of a corporation cannot in many cases be conveniently conducted and managed by the stockholders, for they are often numerous and widely separated; yet they, in reality, compose the body corporate. [Jones v. Williams, et al, 139 Mo. 1, 39 S.W. 486, 490 (1897)]

One of the many definitions given in Black's *Law Dictionary* (fourth edition revised) is that a corporation is:

An artificial person or legal entity created by or under the authority of the laws of a state or nation, composed, in some rare instances, of a single person and his successors, being the incumbents of a particular office, but ordinarily consisting of an association of numerous individuals, who subsist as a body politic under a specific denomination, which is regarded in law as having a personality and existence distinct from that of its several members, and which is, by the same authority, vested with the capacity of continuous succession, irrespective of changes in its membership, either in perpetuity or for a limited term of years, and of acting as a unit or single individual in matters relating to the common purpose of the association, within the scope of the powers and authorities conferred upon such bodies by law (page 409).

A simpler way to describe a corporation is: It is a separate thing, an artificial person or legal entity which you can create by following the steps set out in the statutes of your state.

While these legal definitions are generally approved as correct descriptions of a corporation, it is within the power of the legislature of your state to define a corporation. If an association falls within that definition, the courts will recognize the definition as legally binding. The important thing for you to know is that a corporation is a separate, distinct entity from you, even though you may own substantially all of the stock and conduct most of the activities of the corporation.

Types of Corporations

Corporations fall into the following broad classifications: (1) public, (2) private or profit-making, (3) quasi-

4

public, (4) nonprofit, (5) foreign, and (6) domestic.

A *public* corporation is one created for public purposes only. It is connected with the administration of
the government. Examples are states, school districts,
cities, and counties. *Quasi-public* is a term applied to
corporations which are not strictly public in the sense of
being organized for governmental purposes. Quasi-
public corporations are those which operate by contri-
buting to the comfort, convenience, and welfare of the
general public. Examples are gas, water, electric, and
other utility companies. *Private* corporations are created
for private purposes as distinguished from those purely
public and are generally thought of as business entities
carrying on activities for profit-making purposes. A
profit-making corporation is primarily a business corporation organized with a view toward gains that are to be
distributed among its members. A *nonprofit* corporation,
sometimes referred to as eleemosynary, is one created for
or devoted to charitable purposes or those supported by
charity. *Foreign* corporations are those organized in
another state or country. A *domestic* corporation is one
organized within the state. As we shall see later, it is *not*
generally recommended that you organize your corporation in a foreign state or jurisdiction.

Basically, the character of a corporation is determined by the object of its formation and the nature of its
business. The character of a corporation may not be
changed by calling it something different from that speci-

fied in its articles of incorporation. Because of this requirement, you should make certain that the articles sufficiently describe and define the purposes for which the corporation is established.

Alternative Business Entities Available

When you are considering whether to form a corporation, you should know what options are available and their characteristics as compared to incorporation. Some of the most important items to consider in making a decision include:

1. liability exposure,
2. tax costs and considerations,
3. centralization of management,
4. advantages of raising capital through issuance of stock,
5. ability to attract and keep key personnel through various fringe benefits or participation as stockholders, and
6. the practical convenience of the various forms in which a business might be conducted.

As the risk of potential personal liability increases, whether from the nature of the business or from the extent of your assets, the value of eliminating personal liability increases and the advantage of the corporate form increases. The small expenses involved in setting up a corporation are relatively insignificant when compared with the liability factors.

Other Business Entities

The three business forms of business organization most commonly used are (1) individual proprietorship, (2) partnership, and (3) corporation. Other forms of business organizations are listed and generally described below.

Limited Partnerships. These have all the legal and tax features of partnerships except that the liability of limited partners can be limited to the capital each invests in the venture. These organizations are similar to corporations in the sense that personal liability of the investors is limited. However, the limited partnership is most frequently used solely as a vehicle for investments for capital appreciation.

Combination of Partnership and Corporations. A corporation can be set up to manufacture or perform some business function for which limitation of liability or some other objective makes the corporation particularly suitable. A partnership can sell or perform other associated functions. Such combination of business entities which have common ownership and management requires good faith transactions.

Multiple Corporations. Tax advantages can be achieved through the use of multiple corporations. Professional advice is generally required to comply with tax laws where multiple corporations are utilized by one controlled group.

Incorporate, but Keep Certain Assets out of the Corporation. Frequently it is desirable to keep a patent or piece of real estate out of the corporation and to have a corporation make rental or royalty payments to the individual owner of that property. Expert tax advice is usually required to set up these arrangements.

Corporation Electing Not to Pay Corporate Tax: Sub Chapter S. If there are to be fifteen or less stockholders and very little investment income, it is possible to qualify the corporation under Sub Chapter S of the Internal Revenue Code. This enables the corporation to retain all the legal advantages of limited liability among others, and to avoid income tax at the corporate level.

Factors to Consider in Selection of A Business Entity

No matter what form of business entity you ultimately decide to use, it is important to know what controlling factors to consider. The major items are listed and discussed below.

Simplicity. The individual proprietorship is the least complicated way to operate a business. You simply start a business with no legal formalities. This partially explains why so many people operate this way. A partnership can be uncomplicated—but it can also be complex and hazardous. You can start a partnership with a handshake or with a lengthy written partnership agreement, depending on the nature of the business and the

8

persons involved. Any partner can dissolve a partnership at will in the absence of a contract to the contrary. This allows one partner to freely terminate a partnership without the consent of the other partners. The death of one of the partners automatically ends the partnership. The trend in the business community is usually to incorporate in most business enterprises. Recent changes in state corporation statutes make incorporation simple and economical.

Organizational Flexibility. The corporate form permits great variation in operation and development. For example, greater or lesser powers may be bestowed on a governing board of directors by a larger or smaller number of members. That is, smaller working committees with specified powers may be established for purposes such as overall management on a temporary basis, an executive committee to operate in special fields on a continuing basis, a finance committee, or a retirement committee. Departments may be created, branches established, and offices created at various levels with supervisory personnel below them in any number of levels required by the business. The modern corporate form has developed an almost unlimited flexibility of managerial organization.

Financing. In the early stages of a business enterprise, financing will probably depend on the personal credit of the principals. However, this is generally true in any form of business. When the business accumulates assets and shows earning power, it will establish its own credit without involving the principals. The availability of corporate stock will be important in providing additional capacity to attract financing either through private or public offer of stock.

Continuity. Continuity is assured through the corporate form better than through any other. A partnership terminates upon the death of a partner and a final accounting becomes necessary. This can be a burden during inconvenient times. A corporation continues to exist no matter how many of its directors, officers, or stockholders die. Title to property, contracts, and other rights remain unaffected, and the business can continue to operate. Stock transfers can be accomplished speedily and new elections can be held as often as needed. The corporation is a vehicle ideally suited for continuing a business beyond a single generation, and its advantage grows in importance with the growth of the business.

Transferability of Shares. As a business prospers, there are certain occasions in which the owners may wish to distribute all or part of the ownership to others. This is not feasible in a sole proprietorship, but is easy, and convenient through the corporate form by transfers of stock.

Good Will. If good will is likely to develop into an asset of substantial value, it is advantageous for the corporate form to accumulate good will and maintain public identification.

Compensation Arrangements. The corporate form makes it possible to attract and reward talent with stock options, stock purchases, deferred compensation arrangements, participation of the owners in pension and profit sharing plans, group insurance benefits, and other benefits.

Estate Liquidity. The possible future sale of corporate shares and the possible creation of a public market hold the promise of easing estate liquidity problems. Even when this is not likely to occur, the corporate form may make the way easier to accumulate earnings and pay for insurance to facilitate the redemption of shares owned by a deceased stockholder.

Splitting Income among the Family. A family partnership is a suitable method for splitting income and capital values among children and other members of the family, but the corporate form has this same flexibility. The corporation is also well suited for capital appreciation.

**Advantages of Corporate Entity
over Other Business Entities**

Several factors in deciding on a form of business organization have been discussed, but the following are the most significant reasons for adoption of the corporate form.

11

1. The owners, stockholders, or principals have no individual liability other than the capital contribution in stock payments.

2. Corporations are perpetual.

3. Corporations are a separate entity from the stockholders. They can sue and be sued, and hold and deal in property.

4. Stock can ordinarily be sold or otherwise transferred at will.

5. Corporations can raise capital by the issuance of new stock, bonds, or other securities.

6. A board of directors is the center of authority, acting by majority agreement.

7. As a separate entity, a corporation has credit possibilities apart from stockholders, and stock is sometimes available as collateral.

8. Corporations have flexibility in that the charter and bylaws can be easily changed.

9. The trend in the business world is toward greater use of the corporation. This is a result of the ever increasing exposure to personal liability, the ease with which one can incorporate under the simplified state laws, and the many other advantages of incorporation.

10. The tax advantages of incorporation include the use of a corporation as a tax shelter, wealth building advantages under corporate pension and profit sharing plans, group life, medical, and hospital insurance coverage for owners, deductions for business losses, and others.

Where to Incorporate

Many years ago, it was considered advantageous to incorporate in some state other than your own where there were more liberal laws. This was called "corporate forum shipping." This practice is no longer advisable and has more disadvantages than advantages. Now it is almost universally accepted that the state of principal business activity is the state favored for incorporation. This is true for large corporations and is almost a certainty for small corporations that are not or will not be actively engaged in business activities in many other states. In the case of local business operations, it is especially important to incorporate in your state. And virtually all states have simplified incorporation statutes, most of which are patterned after the Model Business Corporation Act of the Committee on Corporate Laws of the American Bar Association.

Considering current circumstances, incorporation in another state will usually add to organizational and recurring operational costs, including tax costs. A further disadvantage may be the possibility of a suit against the corporation in what will likely be an inconvenient and hostile foreign forum. Moreover, your company will be considered a foreign corporation in the courts of your home state. This could subject you to attachment proceedings (seizure of property by legal authority) and other procedural disadvantages. Also, if you incorporate in another state, you will be required to register in your state as a foreign corporation before you can legitimately carry on a local business in your state. Usually, the expenses to register a foreign corporation to do business in your state are much greater than the cost of forming a corporation there. It follows that the outdated advice to go forum shopping to incorporate could be a mistake and costly to you. For example, in some states the filing fee to register a foreign corporation to do business within the state is over $400. California recently raised this to $550. Most other states are doing the same thing. The filing fee to incorporate in your state is much less.

Over the past 30 years we have seen much greater uniformity in the corporate laws of all states. However, if you still wish to go shopping for a foreign corporate forum, it is to your advantage to acquire good legal advice before making a final decision.

2

Steps in Creating and Organizing Your Corporation

Establishing your corporation is usually a simple matter once you determine the state's requirements. The procedure is set out in each state statute. Most statutes, based on the Model Act, require nothing more than these simple steps:

1. selection of the name,
2. filling out a form of articles of incorporation furnished by the secretary of state or another officer designated to administer corporations,
3. filing the form with the filing fees,
4. getting a corporate kit, and
5. holding an organizational meeting.

The secretary of state or other officer can give you all the necessary forms, and you can purchase a corporate kit or you can make one.

A copy of your state corporation statutes may be obtained in any law library. A summary of each of the state statutes is contained in the *Martindale-Hubbell Law Directory* found in most law libraries. Either write, call, or visit the state office which administers the corporation laws to obtain forms and information on filing fees. Your letter can be based on this sample:

Dear Sir:

I wish to form a new corporation in this state and request that you send me the forms and information necessary to effect a legal incorporation in this state. I also request that you forward me a schedule of all fees required for incorporation.

Almost invariably each state office has several people whose primary responsibilities are to assist in filing these papers and to keep the corporate records of the state. Usually they are helpful and cooperative in giving any information or assistance needed. The following list contains all of the steps necessary to complete your incorporation. Note that some of these steps are not required in all states.

1. *Determine the Availability of Your Corporate Name.* You certainly would not name your corporation General Motors, Inc., A. T. & T., or IBM because these are among the many names already taken. Simply call or write to the secretary of state to see if the name you want to use is available. Most states will give this information on the telephone, others require a letter. If you wish, a name can be reserved by paying a nominal fee, but this is usually a waste of time, money, and effort unless you expect to have some extensive delay in filing. Once you learn that the desired name is available, you simply fill

out the papers and file them. The following forms, which include the essential papers, can be used in getting your new corporation organized.

2. *File the Articles of Incorporation.* All states have forms for completion of these articles. See Form 1, one which is taken from the Model Act and is representative of most states.

Completion of the form is a relatively simple matter, but there are several items you should consider. These suggestions include the practice of most people who form their corporations. The duration is usually filled in as "perpetual." Describe the basic purpose as suggested by the descriptions in Appendix A and add the phrase "and all other acts authorized by law." In some states the filing fee is determined by the aggregate number of shares the corporation is authorized to issue. In these states you should authorize the minimum number on the sliding scale to keep the filing fee as low as possible.

It is important to distinguish *authorized* shares (those you may or may not wish to issue) from *issued* shares (those actually issued by the corporation). In a small corporation you may wish to issue only a few shares in the beginning—perhaps no more than 20 or 200 shares among 10,000 to 50,000 authorized shares. The idea is to have additional authorized shares that can be issued later when other capital is needed in the corporation. You should indicate cumulative voting of shares of stock as

17

authorized, and that there shall be no provisions limiting or denying to shareholders the preemptive right to acquire additional or treasury shares of the corporation. The name of the initial registered agent should be the principal person responsible for the creation and operation of the business.

3. *Pay Filing Fees.* These vary on the average from $10 to about $40. A few states are somewhat higher. Determine from the secretary of state whether payment of any other fees or taxes, and/or whether any other notice, publication, or filing are required in your state.

4. *Hold Organizational Meetings.* Legally, and technically, the certificate of the secretary of state or other approval of the initial corporate papers is considered to be the creation of a corporation. It has a legal existence by virtue of the completion of the statutory requirements and the declaration of the state official that the corporation is in existence. However, in a practical sense, it is necessary to take formal steps to make the corporation an operating entity. This procedure includes the election of officers and directors, the subscription and payment of capital stock, adoption of bylaws, and other steps necessary to provide the legal entity with the capacity to actually transact business. This is accomplished by the holding of formal, organizational meetings. In some states these meetings are held by the incorporators, and in others by the stockholders or the members of the board of

directors listed or designated in the articles of incorporation.

The specific procedural steps usually taken at these meetings include the election of directors, adoption of bylaws, designation of principal corporate office and any branch offices, adoption of the corporate seal and stock certificates, authorizing the issuance of stock, accepting payment of the required amount for commencement of business, designation of official corporate record books, adoption of a plan under Section 1244 of the Internal Revenue Code (see Chapter 4), approval of the filing of the articles of incorporation, and any other appropriate procedural requirements. In some circumstances additional items may be covered at these meetings. However, it is generally preferable to leave the business matters to the board of directors, even though the incorporators, stockholders, and the members of the board of directors may be the same person or persons.

In a small corporation where the incorporators, stockholders, members of the board of directors, and the officers consist of a small group of people, the organizational meeting of the board of directors is usually a formality where the procedures and steps taken at the first meeting of incorporators are approved and the board takes any other action that may be needed. The board of directors should formally approve action taken at any other organizational meetings, and have this approval noted in the minutes of the meeting. The statutes, articles of incorporation, and bylaws should be reviewed to ensure that the board of directors approves all items required.

Generally, the secretary is the person who keeps the corporate books and has the responsibility of preparing proper and appropriate records of the organizational and other meetings. In the event you do not have a corporate kit or you decide to prepare your own, the forms in this book can be adopted as they are or revised for your specific purposes.

5. *Local Filings.* A few states have a provision for filing with local authorities, usually the county or city clerk. This is normally a notice of incorporation to be placed on record by the clerk. When you file with the secretary of state you should ask whether any other formalities are required in your state. This rule of local filings is a holdover from the older statutory enactments and is no longer found in the modern statutes.

6. *Prepare and Approve Bylaws.* The bylaws are extremely important in the sense that they are the governing rules for the internal operations of the corporation. However, it is a general practice in a small corporation to grant extensive powers and authority to the officers and directors for carrying on the business operations of the corporation. This makes it unnecessary to have frequent or regular formal meetings of the board of directors or

stockholders. Most corporate kits have a suggested form for bylaws providing for full and complete powers and authority in the officers and directors.

7. *Obtain Corporate Kit.* Most kits contain a corporate seal, stock register, stock certificate book, bylaws, and minute book. These can be purchased at most large stationery stores or you can prepare one. The following forms will be useful in preparing your kit.

FORM 1: Articles of Incorporation

We, the undersigned, natural persons of the age of _____ years or more, acting as incorporators of a corporation under the laws of the state of _____ , adopt the following articles of incorporation for such corporation:

First: The name of the corporation is _____ .

Second: The period of its duration is _____ .

Third: The purpose or purposes for which the corporation is organized are _____ .

Fourth: The aggregate number of shares which the corporation shall have authority to issue is _____ .

Fifth: The corporation will not commence business until at least _____ _____ Dollars have been received by it as consideration for the issuance of shares.

Sixth: Cumulative voting of shares of stock [is], [is not] authorized.

Seventh: Provisions limiting or denying to shareholders the preemptive right to acquire additional or treasury shares of the corporation are: _____ _____ .

Eighth: Provisions for the regulation of the internal affairs of the corporation are: _____ .

Ninth: The address of the initial registered office of the corporation is _____ , and the name of its initial registered agent at such address is _____ .

Tenth: Address of the principal place of business is _____ _____ .

Eleventh: The number of directors constituting the initial board of directors of the corporation is _____ , and the names and addresses of the persons who are to serve as directors until the first annual meeting of shareholders or until their successors are elected and shall qualify are:

Name	Address
_____	_____
_____	_____
_____	_____

Twelfth: The name and address of each incorporator is:

Name   Address

_____   _____
_____   _____
_____   _____

(Date)   _____
                                        _____
                                        _____
(Verification)   Incorporators

FORM 2: Waiver of Notice of the Organization Meeting

We, the undersigned, being all the incorporators [and/or the members of the board of directors] named in the Articles of Incorporation of the above corporation [and/or the stockholders], hereby agree and consent that the organization meeting thereof be held on the date and the time and place stated below and hereby waive all notice of such meeting and of any adjournment thereof.

Place of Meeting: _____
Date of Meeting: _____
Time of Meeting: _____

(Date)   _____
                                        (Signatures)
                                        _____

                                        _____

FORM 3: Minutes of the Organization Meeting

The organization meeting of the incorporators [and/or the stock-holders and/or the members of the board of directors] of _____ was held at _____ on _____ at _____.

The following were present: _____

_____

_____

being all the incorporators [and/or the stockholders and/or the members of the board of directors] of the corporation.

_____ was appointed chairman of the meeting and _____ _____ was appointed secretary.

The secretary then presented and read to the meeting the waiver of notice of the meeting, subscribed by all the persons named in the Articles of Incorporation, and it was ordered that it be appended to the minutes of the meeting.

The secretary then presented and read to the meeting a copy of the Articles of Incorporation and reported that on _____ the original thereof was filed in the office of the Secretary of State of this state. The copy of the Articles of Incorporation was ordered appended to the minutes of the meeting.

The chairman then stated that nominations were in order for election of directors of the corporation to hold office until the first annual meeting of stockholders and until their successors shall be elected and shall qualify.

The following persons were nominated: _____

_____

_____

No further nominations being made, nominations were closed and a vote was taken. After the vote had been counted, the chairman declared that the foregoing named nominees were elected directors of the corporation.

The secretary then presented to the meeting a proposed form of bylaws which were read to the meeting, considered, and upon motion duly made, seconded and carried, were adopted as and for the bylaws of the corporation and ordered appended to the minutes of the meeting.

Upon motion duly made, seconded, and unanimously carried, it was

Further Resolved, that the specimen stock certificate presented to the

24

meeting be and hereby is adopted as the form of certificate of stock to be issued to represent shares in the corporation;

Further Resolved, that the corporate record book, including the stock transfer ledger, be and hereby is adopted as the record book, stock transfer book, and ledger of the corporation;

Further resolved, that the board of directors be and hereby is authorized to issue the unsubscribed capital stock of the corporation at such time and in such amounts as it shall determine, and to accept the payment thereof, in cash or services or such other property as the board may deem necessary for the business of the corporation;

Further Resolved, that the corporate seal presented to the meeting by the secretary be and the same is hereby adopted as the seal of the corporation;

Further Resolved, that the corporation be and hereby is authorized and directed to accept the payment of capital required for the commencement of business, and that the same be properly reflected upon the books and records of the corporation;

Further Resolved, that the principal office of the corporation be and hereby is designated as _____ and the board of directors is hereby authorized to change said designation as it deems proper and it may designate branch offices from time to time as it shall, in its judgment, determine to be necessary and proper;

Further Resolved, that a plan for the issuance of common stock of the corporation to qualify under the provisions of Section 1244 of the Internal Revenue Code, which plan was read to the meeting, be and the same is hereby adopted, approved, and confirmed by the corporation, and the officers and directors of the corporation are hereby authorized and directed to take all steps, procedures, and action necessary to implement the plan;

Further Resolved, that all other actions, notifications, publications, filings, and any other procedural requirements for the full authorization of this corporation to commence the business for which it was created be completed by the secretary, and that a record thereof be filed in the corporate records of the corporation.

Upon motion duly made, seconded, and carried, it was

Resolved, that the signing of these minutes shall constitute full ratification thereof and waiver of notice of the meeting by the signatories.

There being no further business before the meeting, on motion duly made, seconded, and carried, the meeting adjourned.

(Date)

_____
Chairman

_____
Secretary

FORM 4: Call and Waiver of Notice of Organizational Meeting

We, the undersigned, being all of the directors [and/or the incorporators and/or the stockholders] of _____ , hereby call the organizational meeting of the corporation, to consider and transact any business whatsoever that may be brought before the meeting, and we hereby fix ____ _____ at _____ as the place of the meeting, and hereby waive any and all requirements by statute, bylaws, or otherwise, as to notice of the time, place, and purposes of the meeting, and consent that the meeting be held at the time and place set out above and to the transaction thereat or at any adjournment thereof of any business whatsoever that may be brought before the meeting, including, without any limitation on the scope of the foregoing, the adoption of bylaws, election of officers, and authorization of issuance of stock.

(Date)   (Signatures)

26

FORM 5: Minutes of the First Meeting of the Board of Directors

Pursuant to _____ , the Board of Directors of _____ _____ , elected at the organizational meeting of the incorporation on _____ , assembled and held its first meeting at [place] on [date] at [time].

Present at the meeting were _____ , _____ , and _____ , being all of the directors.

_____ called the meeting to order, and on motion duly made and seconded, he was appointed temporary chairman, and _____ _____ was appointed temporary secretary.

The election of officers was thereupon declared to be in order. The following were named and duly elected: _____ , president; _____ , vice-president; and _____ , as secretary-treasurer. _____ took the chair and presided at the meeting.

The secretary presented a form of bylaws (adopted by the incorporators and/or the stockholders) for the regulation of the affairs of the corporation, which were read section by section.

On motion duly made, seconded, and carried, it was

Resolved, that the bylaws submitted at and read to this meeting be, and the same hereby are, approved as and for the bylaws of this corporation, and that the secretary be, and she hereby is, instructed to certify the bylaws and cause the same to be inserted in the minute book of this corporation, and to certify a copy of the bylaws, which shall be kept at the principal office of this corporation and open to inspection by stockholders at all reasonable times during office hours.

On motion duly made, seconded, and carried, it was

Resolved, that the seal (adopted by the incorporators and/or the stockholders), an impression of which is herewith affixed, be adopted as the corporate seal of the corporation.

[corporate seal]

The secretary was authorized and directed to procure the proper corporate books.

On motion duly made, seconded, and carried, it was

Resolved, that [name of bank] of the City of _____ , State of
_____ , be, and it is, hereby selected as a depositary for the money,
funds, and credits of this corporation and that _____ and
_____ be, and they are authorized and empowered to draw
checks on the above depositary, against the account for this corporation
with the depositary, and to endorse in the name of this corporation and
receive payment of all checks, drafts, and commercial papers payable to
this corporation either as payee or endorsee;

Further Resolved, that the certification of the secretary of this corporation as to the election and appointment of persons so authorized to sign
such checks and as to the signatures of such persons shall be binding on
this corporation;

Further Resolved, that the secretary of this corporation be, and she
hereby is, authorized and directed to deliver to said bank a copy of these
resolutions properly certified by her.

On motion duly made, seconded, and carried, it was

Resolved, that the principal office of the corporation for the transaction
of its business be, and it hereby is, fixed at _____ .

Further Resolved, that the specimen stock certificate presented to this
meeting be and hereby is approved as the form of certificate of stock to be
issued to represent shares in the corporation;

Further Resolved, that the corporate record book, including the stock
transfer ledger, be and hereby is approved as the record book and stock
transfer ledger of the corporation;

Further Resolved, that the treasurer of the corporation be and hereby is
authorized to pay all charges and expenses incident to or arising out of the
organization of the corporation and to reimburse any person who has
made any disbursement therefor;

Further Resolved, that all actions taken at the organizational meeting of
the incorporators, and/or the stockholders, and/or the members of the
board of directors designated in the Articles of Incorporation, as reflected
by the minutes of said meeting, be and they are hereby ratified, confirmed,
and approved;

Further Resolved, that the officers of this corporation take such other procedural action as may be necessary for this corporation to commence the transaction of business in this state.

There being no further business, the meeting was adjourned.

_____
Secretary

FORM 6: Bylaws

Article 1: Offices

The principal office of the corporation shall be located at _____
_____ . The board of directors shall have the power and authority to
establish and maintain branch or subordinate offices at any other location
either within this state or in any other state or country.

Article 2: Stockholders

Section 1. Annual Meetings: The annual meeting of the stockholders
shall be held on the ____ day of the month of ____ in each year, beginning
with the year 19__ , at the hour of ____ o'clock, for the purpose of electing
directors and for the transaction of such other business as may come before
the meeting. If the day fixed for the annual meeting shall be a legal holiday
in the state of incorporation, such meeting shall be held on the next
succeeding business day. If the election of directors is not held on the day
designated herein for any annual meeting of the shareholders, or at any
adjournment thereof, the board of directors shall cause the election to be
held at a special meeting of the stockholders as soon thereafter as is
convenient.

Section 2. Special Meetings: Special meetings of the stockholders, for
any purpose or purposes, unless otherwise prescribed by statute, may be
called by the president or by the board of directors, and shall be called by
the president at the request of the holders of not less than ____ percent of
all the outstanding shares of the corporation entitled to vote at the meeting.

Section 3: Place of Meeting: The board of directors may designate any
place within the state of incorporation or within any other state as the
place of meeting for any annual meeting or for any special meeting called
by the board of directors. A waiver of notice signed by all stockholders
entitled to vote at a meeting may designate any place, either within the state
of incorporation or in any other state, as the place for the holding of such
meeting. If no designation is made, or if a special meeting is otherwise
called, the place of the meeting shall be the principal office of the corporation as designated pursuant to Article 1.

Section 4. Notice of Meeting: Written or printed notice stating the place,

30

day, and hour of the meeting and, in case of a special meeting, the purpose or purposes for which the meeting is called, shall be delivered not less than _____ nor more than _____ days before the date of the meeting, either personally or by mail, by or at the direction of the president, or the secretary, or the officer or persons calling the meeting, to each shareholder of record entitled to vote at such meeting. If mailed, such notice shall be deemed to be delivered when deposited in the United States mail, addressed to the shareholder at his address as it appears on the stock transfer books of the corporation with postage thereon prepaid. Notice of each meeting shall also be mailed to holders of stock not entitled to vote, if any, as herein provided, but lack of such notice shall not affect the legality of any meeting otherwise properly called and noticed.

Section 5. Closing of Stock Transfer Books: For the purpose of determining stockholders entitled to notice of, or to vote at, any meeting of stockholders or any adjournment thereof, or stockholders entitled to receive payment of any dividend, or to make a determination of shareholders for any other purpose, the board of directors of the corporation may provide that the stock transfer books shall be closed for a stated period, but not to exceed _____ days. If the stock transfer books shall be closed for the purpose of determining stockholders entitled to notice of, or to vote at, a meeting of stockholders, such books shall be closed for at least _____ days preceding such meeting. In lieu of closing the stock transfer books, the board of directors may fix in advance a date as the record date for any such determination of stockholders, such date in any event to be not more than _____ days, and in case of a meeting of stockholders, not less than _____ days, prior to the date on which the particular action requiring such determination of stockholders is to be taken.

If the stock transfer books are not closed and no record date is fixed for the determination of stockholders entitled to notice of, or to vote at, a meeting of stockholders, or of stockholders entitled to receive payment of a dividend, the date that notice of the meeting is mailed or the date on which the resolution of the board of directors declaring such dividend is adopted, as the case may be, shall be the record date for such determination of stockholders. When a determination of stockholders entitled to vote at any meeting of stockholders has been made as provided in this section, such determination shall apply to any adjournment thereof except where the

31

determination has been made through the closing of the stock transfer books and the stated period of closing has expired.

Section 6. Quorum Requirements for Stockholder Meetings: A majority of the outstanding shares of the corporation entitled to vote, represented in person or by proxy, shall constitute a quorum at a meeting of stockholders. If less than a majority of such outstanding shares are represented at a meeting, a majority of the shares so represented may adjourn the meeting from time to time without notice. At such adjourned meeting at which a quorum is present or represented, any business may be transacted that might have been transacted at the meeting as originally notified. The stockholders present at a duly organized meeting may continue to transact business until adjournment, notwithstanding the withdrawal of enough stockholders to leave less than a quorum.

Section 7. Voting of Shares: Subject to the provisions of any applicable law, the Articles of Incorporation or these bylaws concerning cumulative voting, each outstanding share entitled to vote shall be entitled to one vote on each matter submitted to a vote at a meeting of stockholders.

Section 8. Proxies: At all meetings of stockholders, a stockholder may vote by proxy executed in writing by the stockholder or by his duly authorized attorney in fact. Such proxy shall be filed with the secretary of the corporation before or at the time of the meeting. No proxy shall be valid after _____ months from the date of its execution unless otherwise provided in the proxy.

Article 3: Board of Directors

Section 1. Powers and Duties: The business and affairs of the corporation shall be managed by its board of directors.

Section 2. Qualifications of Members: The number of directors of the corporation shall be _____ . Directors shall be elected at the annual meeting of stockholders, and the term of office of each director shall be until the next annual meeting of stockholders and the election and qualification of his successor. Directors need not be residents of the state of incorporation, but shall be stockholders of the corporation.

Section 3. Regular Meetings: A regular meeting of the board of directors shall be held without notice other than this bylaw immediately after, and at the same place as, the annual meeting of stockholders. The board of directors may provide, by resolution, the time and place for holding additional regular meetings without other notice than such resolution. Additional regular meetings shall be held at the principal office of the corporation in the absence of any designation in the resolution.

Section 4. Special Meetings: Special meetings of the board of directors may be called by, or at the request of, the president or any two directors, and shall be held at the principal office of the corporation or at such other place as the directors may determine.

Section 5. Notice: Notice of any special meeting shall be given at least _____ hours before the time fixed for the meeting, by written notice delivered personally or mailed to each director at his business address or by telegram. If mailed, such notice shall be deemed to be delivered when deposited in the United States mail so addressed, with postage thereon prepaid, not less than _____ days prior to the commencement of the above stated notice period. If notice is given by telegram, such notice shall be deemed to be delivered when the telegram is delivered to the telegraph company. Any director may waive notice of any meeting. The attendance of a director at a meeting shall constitute a waiver of notice of such meeting, except where a director attends a meeting for the express purpose of objecting to the transaction of any business because the meeting is not lawfully called or convened. Neither the business to be transacted at, nor the purpose of, any regular or special meeting of the board of directors need be specified in the notice or waiver of notice of such meeting.

Section 6. Quorum: A majority of the number of directors fixed by these bylaws shall constitute a quorum for the transaction of business at any meeting of the board of directors, but if less than such majority is present at a meeting, a majority of the directors present may adjourn the meeting from time to time without further notice.

Section 7. Board of Director Decisions: The act of the majority of the directors present at a meeting at which a quorum is present shall be the act of the board of directors.

Section 8. Compensation: By resolution of the board of directors, the directors may be paid their expenses, if any, of attendance of each meeting of the board of directors, and may be paid a fixed sum for attendance at each meeting of the board of directors or a stated salary as director. No such payment shall preclude any director from serving the corporation in any other capacity and receiving compensation therefor.

33

Article 4: Officers

Section 1. Number and Vacancies: The officers of the corporation shall be a president, one or more vice-presidents, a secretary, and a treasurer, each of whom shall be elected by the board of directors.

Such other officers and assistant officers as may be deemed necessary may be elected or appointed by the board of directors. Any two or more offices may be held by the same person, except the office of president. A vacancy in any office because of death, resignation, removal, disqualification, or otherwise, may be filled by the board of directors for the unexpired portion of the term.

Section 2. Election, Term of Office, and Removal: The officers of the corporation to be elected by the board of directors shall be elected annually at the first meeting of the board of directors held after each annual meeting of the stockholders. If the election of officers is not held at such meeting, such election shall be held as soon thereafter as is convenient. Each officer shall hold office until his successor has been duly elected and qualifies, or until his death, or until he resigns or is removed in the manner hereinafter provided. Any officer or agent elected or appointed by the board of directors may be removed by the board of directors whenever in its judgment the best interests of the corporation would be served thereby, but such removal shall be without prejudice to the contract rights, if any, of the person so removed.

Section 3. Salaries: The salaries of the officers shall be fixed from time to time by the board of directors, and no officer shall be prevented from receiving such salary by reason of the facat that he is also a director of the corporation.

Section 4. Powers and Duties: The powers and duties of the several officers shall be as provided from time to time by resolution or other directive of the board of directors. In the absence of such provisions, the respective officers shall have the powers and shall discharge the duties customarily and usually held and performed by like officers of corporations similar in organization and business purposes to this corporation.

Article 5: Conduct of Business

Section 1. Contracts: The board of directors may authorize any officer or officers, agent or agents, to enter into any contract or execute and deliver any instrument in the name of, and on behalf of, the corporation, and such authority may be general or confined to specific instances.

Section 2. Loans: No loans shall be contracted on behalf of the corporation and no evidence of indebtedness shall be issued in its name unless authorized by a resolution of the board of directors. Such authority may be general or confined to specific instances.

Section 3. Checks, Drafts, or Orders: All checks, drafts, or other orders for the payment of money, notes, or other evidences of indebtedness issued in the name of the corporation shall be signed by such officer or officers, agent or agents, of the corporation and in such manner as shall from time to time be determined by resolution of the board of directors.

Section 4. Deposits: All funds of the corporation not otherwise employed shall be deposited from time to time to the credit of the corporation in such banks, trust companies, or other depositaries as the board of directors may select.

Article 6: Corporate Stock and Stock Transfers

Section 1. Certificates for Shares of Stock: Certificates representing shares of the corporation shall be in such form as shall be determined by the board of directors. Such certificates shall be signed by the president, or a vice-president, and by the secretary or an assistant secretary. All certificates for shares shall be consecutively numbered or otherwise identified. The name and address of the person to whom the shares represented thereby are issued, with the number of shares and date of issue, shall be entered on the stock transfer books of the corporation. All certificates surrendered to the corporation for transfer shall be canceled and no new certificate shall be issued until the former certificate for the like number of shares shall have been surrendered or canceled, except that in case of a lost, destroyed, or mutilated certificate a new one may be issued therefor on such terms and indemnity to the corporation as the board of directors may prescribe.

Section 2. Transfer of Shares of Stock on Books of Record: The transfer of shares of stock of the corporation shall be made in the manner required by law, and pursuant to procedures established by the board of directors. The corporation shall maintain stock transfer books, and any transfer shall be registered thereon only on request and surrender of the stock certificate representing the transferred shares, duly endorsed. The corporation shall have the absolute right to recognize as the owner of any shares of stock issued by it, the person or persons in whose name the certificate representing such shares stands according to the books of the corporation for all proper corporate purposes, including the voting of the shares represented by the certificate at a regular or special meeting of stockholders, and the issuance and payment of dividends on such shares.

Article 7: Fiscal Year

The fiscal year of the corporation shall be _____ .

Article 8: Dividends

The board of directors may from time to time declare, and the corporation may pay, dividends on its outstanding shares in the manner and on the terms and conditions provided by law and its Articles of Incorporation.

Article 9: Seal

The board of directors shall provide a corporate seal, which shall be circular in form and shall have inscribed thereon the name of the corporation and the state of incorporation and the words "Corporate Seal." The seal shall be stamped or affixed to such documents as may be prescribed by law or custom or by the board of directors.

Article 10: Waiver of Notice

Whenever any notice is required to be given to any stockholder or director of the corporation under the provisions of these bylaws or under the provisions of the Articles of Incorporation or under the provisions of law, a waiver thereof in writing, signed by the person or persons entitled to such notice, whether before or after the time stated therein, shall be deemed equivalent to the giving of such notice.

Article 11: Amendments to These Bylaws

These bylaws may be altered, amended, or repealed and new bylaws may be adopted by the board of directors at any regular or special meeting of the board provided, however, that the number of directors shall not be increased or decreased, nor shall the provisions of Article Two, concerning the stockholders, be substantially altered without the prior approval of the stockholders at a regular or special meeting of the stockholders, or by written consent. Changes in, and additions to, the bylaws by the board of directors shall be reported to the stockholders at their next regular meeting and shall be subject to the approval or disapproval of the stockholders at such meeting. If no action is then taken by the stockholders on a change in, or addition to, the bylaws, such change or addition shall be deemed to be fully approved and ratified by the stockholders.

FORM 7: Notice of Regular Meeting of the Board of Directors

Notice is hereby given that the regular [annual] meeting of the board of directors of _____ is hereby called to be held at [place] on [date] at [time], which meeting shall be for the purpose of _____
_____ .

(Date)   _____
                                                                 Secretary

FORM 8: Waiver of Notice of Regular Meeting of the Board of Directors

The undersigned members of the board of directors of _____ waive notice of the next regular meeting of the board and consent and agree that a meeting of the board of directors may be held at the office of the company, [address], at [time], on [date], for the purpose of transacting all business properly presented to the meeting.

(Date)   (Signatures)

FORM 9: Notice of Special Meeting of the Board of Directors

Please take notice that a special meeting of the board of directors of _____ will be held at the office of the company at [time] on [date] at [address], for the purpose of _____ .

(Date)   _____
                                                                        Secretary

FORM 10: Waiver of Notice of Special Meeting of the Board of Directors

    We, the undersigned, being all of the directors of _____ , a corporation organized and existing under the laws of the State of _____ , desiring to hold a special meeting of the directors of the corporation, hereby severally waive notice and publication of notice of such meeting, and we hereby severally consent and agree to the holding of such meeting of the directors of the corporation at [time] on [date] at [address], for the consideration and transaction of a proposition to _____ and for the transaction of any other business that may be legally done or brought up at the meeting, and we hereby further severally agree that any proceedings and any and all business transacted at this meeting and at any meeting or meetings to which the meeting may be adjourned, shall be as valid and legal, and as of the same force and effect, as if the meeting were held after due notice was given and published.

(Date)   (Signatures)

FORM 11: Notice of Adjourned Meeting of the Board of Directors

To: _____ , Director

    You are hereby notified that the meeting of the board of directors of _____ held at [time] on [date] at [address] was adjourned until [time] at [date], at the same location.

(Date)   _____
                                                                               Secretary

FORM 12: Minutes of Special Meeting of the Board of Directors

The board of directors met pursuant to _____ in special meeting in the office of the corporation, _____ .

The meeting was called to order by the president, _____ , and directors _____ and _____ , consisting of all of the members of the board of directors, and all being present, the board commenced business.

The secretary then presented the _____ pursuant to which the meeting was held. There being no objections, it was ordered to be entered into the minutes.

The president then presented to the board the subject about which the meeting was called, to wit: _____ .

The following action was taken: _____ .

There being no further business, the meeting was adjourned.

(Date)

_____
Secretary

FORM 13: Notice of Regular [or Special] Meeting of Stockholders

Notice is hereby given that _____ meeting of the stockholders of _____ , a corporation organized and existing under the laws of the State of _____ , will be held at the office of the corporation, at [time] on [date] at [address], for the purpose of _____ .

(Date)

_____
Secretary

FORM 14: Notice of Annual Meeting of Stockholders

Notice is hereby given that the annual meeting of the stockholders of _____ will be held at the office of the corporation, _____ _____ , on [date] at [time].

Business to be transacted shall include the following items:
1. To elect directors for the ensuing year.
2. To receive and consider the financial statements and the reports of the affairs of the corporation for the year 19__ .
3. To transact such other business as may properly come before the meeting.

(Date)

_____
Secretary

FORM 15: Waiver of Notice of Meeting of Stockholders

We, the undersigned stockholders of _____ , a corporation organized and existing under the laws of the State of _____ , each entitled to vote the number of shares set opposite his name, do hereby waive notice of a _____ meeting of the stockholders of the said corporation at [time] on [date] at [address], for the purpose of _____ _____ .

This waiver of notice of meeting shall be filed with the corporate books and records and made a part of the minutes of the meeting.

(Date)

Stockholder	Number of Shares
_____	_____
_____	_____
_____	_____
_____	_____
_____	_____

FORM 16: Proxy

I, _____ , do hereby constitute and appoint _____
_____ as attorney and agent for me, and in my name, place, and stead, to
vote as my proxy at any stockholders' meetings to be held between the date
of this proxy and _____ , 19__ , unless sooner revoked, with
full power to cast the number of votes that all my shares of stock
in _____ should entitle me to cast as if I were then personally present, and authorize _____ to act for me and in my
name and stead as fully as I could act if I were present, giving
to _____ , attorney and agent, full power of substitution
and revocation.

In witness whereof, I have executed this proxy on _____ ,
19__ .

_____
Stockholder

FORM 17: Resignation of Officers and Directors

We, the undersigned, hereby tender our resignations as officers and
directors of _____ to take effect immediately.

(Date)   (Signatures)

FORM 18: Minutes of Annual Meeting of Stockholders

The annual meeting of the stockholders of the corporation was held at [time] on [date] at [address].

The meeting was called to order by _____ , the president of the corporation.

The secretary then reported that the meeting had been called pursuant to a notice of meeting [or waiver of notice] thereof in accordance with the bylaws. It was ordered that a copy of the notice and waiver of notice be appended to the minutes of the meeting.

The secretary then read the roll of stockholders from the stock transfer ledger. The following stockholders were present in person or by proxy:

Stockholder	Shares	In Person	By Proxy
_____	_____	_____	_____
_____	_____	_____	_____
_____	_____	_____	_____

The chairman stated that a majority of the total number of shares issued and outstanding was represented and that the meeting was complete and ready to transact any business before it. It was ordered that proxies be appended to the minutes of the meeting.

The president then gave a general report of the business and finances of the corporation and the secretary reported the following changes of stockholders since the last such report: _____ .

The chairman then stated that the election of directors of the corporation was now in order. The following were nominated as directors: _____

_____ .

A ballot was taken, the vote was canvassed and the foregoing nominees were duly elected directors of the corporation to serve until the next annual meeting of stockholders or until their successors are elected.

The following action was taken at the meeting: _____ .

There being no further business, the meeting was, on motion, adjourned.

(Date)   _____
                                                  Secretary

Ratification: We, the undersigned shareholders, or assignees thereof, have read the minutes and do hereby approve, ratify, and confirm all business transacted as reported herein.

(Signatures)

The following have been appended to the minutes: _____
_____ .

FORM 19: Section 1244 Plan for Issuance of Common Stock

The board of directors of _____ deem it advisable and in the best interest of the corporation to offer for sale and issue shares of common stock to shareholders under and pursuant to the provisions of Section 1244 of the Internal Revenue Code of 1954, as amended, in such a manner as to qualify all shares held by qualified stockholders so that the shares shall receive the benefits of the Code.

1. The corporation is a domestic corporation and is a "small business corporation" as defined in Section 1244 of the Code. The stock to be issued pursuant to this plan is common stock.

2. This offer to sell and issue shares of common stock shall terminate no later than two years from the date this plan is approved and adopted by the board of directors of the corporation. The corporation shall not make any subsequent offering of shares of common stock or securities convertible into common stock prior to the expiration date specified herein.

3. Stock issued hereunder shall be in exchange for money or other property except for stock, securities, or services. Stock issued hereunder shall not be in return for services rendered or to be rendered to, or for the benefit of, the corporation.

4. No stock shall be issued under this plan prior to the adoption of this plan.

5. There is not now outstanding any prior offering of the corporation to sell or issue any of its stock.

6. The sum of the aggregate amount which may be offered under this plan, plus the aggregate amount of money and other property received by the corporation for shares of common stock as a contribution to capital and as paid-in surplus, does not exceed $500,000.

7. The sum of the aggregate amount which may be offered under this plan, plus the equity capital of the corporation, does not exceed $1,000,000.

8. No stock offered hereunder shall be issued on the exercise of a stock right, stock warrant, or stock option, unless such right, warrant, or option is applicable solely to unissued stock offered under the plan and is exercised during the period of the plan.

9. The date of adoption of this plan is _____ .

The officers of the corporation are hereby authorized and directed to offer, sell, and issue as many shares of common stock and at such prices, payable in cash or other property, other than stock, securities, or services, as they shall deem to be in the interest of the corporation.

It is the purpose and intent of the corporation to comply with the provisions of Section 1244 of the Internal Revenue Code, as amended, and this plan shall be interpreted and construed in a manner as shall enable the corporation to qualify as a plan meeting the requirements of said Code and as will enable the shares of common stock issued thereunder to qualify as "Section 1244 stock," as defined in the Code.

(Date)
                                        _____
                                            Chairman

Attest: _____
            Secretary

Approved and adopted by the board of directors on the ____ day of _____ , 19__ .

3

Legal Principles Governing Corporations

Corporate Entity

For most purposes, a corporation is an entity distinct from its individual members or stockholders who, as natural persons, are merged in the corporate identity. The corporation's identity remains unchanged and unaffected by changes in its individual membership. By the very nature of a corporation, its property is vested in the corporation itself and not the stockholders. The stockholders, as such, do not have the power to represent the corporation or act for it in relation to its ordinary business, nor ordinarily are they personally liable for the acts and obligations of the corporation. In no legal sense can the business of a corporation be said to be that of its individual stockholders or officers. The corporate entity is distinct even if all or a majority of its stock is owned by a single individual or corporation, or if the corporation is a so-called "close" or "family" corporation. Thus, the ownership of all shares of stock of a corporation by one individual does not avoid the separate identity between the corporation and the individual.

The rules above are subject to the important exception that, since the rules are for the purpose of convenience and to serve the ends of justice, the courts will, in pursuing those ends, treat the stockholders or officers as identical. In other words, the courts will pierce the fiction of or ignore the corporate entity where justice requires it. For example, in cases where individual stockholders or officers are involved in clear fraud, in a cover for fraud or illegality, in an injust work, conspiracy, debt avoidance, or hidden assets, and similar "bad faith" activities, the courts will generally grant relief to any injured party. Where the corporation is formed to accomplish a fraud or other illegal acts, the fiction will be disregarded by the courts and the acts of the real parties dealt with as though no corporation exists. Where a corporation is formed for such a purpose, each individual defrauded may sue the officers or other participants. Stated in realistic and practical terms, the separate entity rule applies to honest, "good faith" transactions, but courts will not permit dishonest persons to use a corporate entity to avoid the obligations arising from their personal, wrongful activities.

Incorporation and Organization

It is well established in law that no corporation can exist without the consent or grant of the sovereign, or the State. The power to create corporations is one of the

attributes of sovereignty. This power is a legislative function. The laws, rules, regulations, and procedures for
creating a corporation are established by the legislature
through the enactment of statutes. Implementation of
these procedures is a function of the executive branch of
the state and is usually delegated to the office of the
secretary of state or some other administrative officer.
The federal government has power to create corporations, but those federal laws are not applicable to our
discussions.

Purposes

It is common for the general corporation laws of
each state to provide for the formation of a corporation
for any lawful business purpose or purposes. Naturally,
one may not legally form a corporation and use it for the
purpose of conducting illegal activities or other purposes
contrary to the laws. However, a corporation may be
legally organized for the specific purpose and intent of
escaping or limiting personal liability of the individual.
In fact, this is one of the primary purposes for forming
many private corporations. An honest, law-abiding person may form a private corporation and carry on honest,
lawful business activities and escape personal liability. A
"bad faith" formation of a corporation to carry on fraudulent, dishonest, or unlawful activities will not be
approved by the courts. For our purposes, we will assume
honest, law-abiding intent, motives, and activities.

Incorporators and Members

Practically all of the state statutes require a private corporation to be formed by natural persons of legal age. Some laws require the incorporators, or a certain number of them, to be residents of the state. This requirement must be complied with to create a valid and lawful corporation. Although one corporation, under some of these statutes, may not create another corporation, it is usually considered permissible for individual stockholders or officers to create another separate corporation with their first corporation allowed to own all of the stock of the second. However, as previously stated, this device can be used only for lawful, honest purposes and not for fraud or other unlawful purpose. Recently, some states have changed the statutes to permit one corporation to form another. Probably most states will follow this trend by enacting these provisions within a few years.

Articles of Incorporation

The contents of the articles of incorporation are determined by the local statutes. Most modern statutes, based on the Model Corporation Act, require the following items in the articles:

1. Name of the corporation
2. Period of duration
3. Purpose or purposes for which the corporation is being organized
4. Number, amount, description, and nature of shares of

stock authorized

5. Names and addresses of officers, directors, incorporators, and resident agent (See Form 1).

The requirements of the statutes as to the form and contents of the articles of incorporation must be substantially complied with. The courts have not hesitated to declare attempted incorporations invalid for failure to do so. If the statute requires the name of a corporation to be stated in its articles, omission of that name can be fatal. In actual practice, the secretary of state or other official who files the papers will usually request that the correct name be shown before the papers are officially recorded.

The laws usually require a statement in the articles concerning the purpose or purposes for which the corporation is formed. Provisions of this kind must be substantially complied with—vague or general specifications of purposes are not sufficient. The character of a corporation is usually determined by the objective of its formation and the nature of its business as stated in its articles. The statutes usually require that the articles be signed by the incorporator(s). It is generally a simple matter to comply with the formal requirements of the statutes because most of the states have simple procedures.

Although procedural requirements for incorporation may differ from state to state, the authorization statutes are of three main classes, (1) those of a general nature giving blanket authority (the right to do every lawful business act), (2) those allowing corporate existence for a specific purpose, and (3) those pertaining to banking, insurance, and similar fields affected with the public interest. To ease the preparation of articles, generally the corporation is vested with all of the normal incidents of the business world. Therefore, it is not necessary to amend the articles to authorize the corporation to engage in other specific activities. See Appendix A for suggested statements of purposes.

After the articles have been completed in accordance with the requirements, they must be filed in the appropriate state office. It is very important to check the statutes and make certain the articles are filed in the correct office, otherwise the incorporation may not be valid. Some of the statutes provide that after the articles have been filed, they shall be recorded, or a certified copy of them shall be filed with the secretary of state, or that a license or certificate shall be obtained from some public officer. In most states the officer who files the articles performs only routine duties, and if the articles are in proper form, he or she must file them. If they are not in conformity with the statutes, he or she must refuse to file them. The officer may, of course, refuse to file articles which indicate that the purposes of the corporation are unlawful or unauthorized. All states require payment of a filing fee. This is a prerequisite for the creation of a lawful corporation.

Most state officers and their employees are cooperative and willing to assist in supplying all information needed to complete the papers required to incorporate. The secretary of state is generally an elective office, and you will find most of these elected officers eager to please you and all other voters and taxpayers. Moreover, you and all other taxpayers pay their salary and expenses in order to render this service to you.

Where Organization Meetings May Be Held

The term "organized" or "organization" generally means the election of officers, the subscription and payment of the capital stock, the adoption of bylaws, and other steps endowing the corporation with the capacity to transact business. Under some statutes these acts must be carried out before the corporation can legally conduct business, and these acts or functions should be performed in the state of incorporation. The articles of incorporation should be accepted by the board of directors, and the first meeting held for the purpose of organizing the corporation and electing its officers within the limits of the state creating it.

It has been held by the courts that an attempted organization of the corporation outside the state is illegal. It has also been held that the votes and proceedings of persons professing to act in the capacity of corporators, when assembled outside the bounds of the state granting the charter, may be invalid. However, most states have recently changed these rules by statute which permit meetings outside the state of incorporation with a prerequisite that the bylaws expressly provide for such meetings.

Most statutes require that notice of the organization meeting be given to the stockholders, but such a requirement is subject to waiver. They are the only persons interested in the results obtained by giving the required notice. While the statute gives the shareholders the legal right to receive a notice of the meeting, they may simply waive the required notice by attending.

Subscription to, Issuance of, and Payment for Stock

When forming a corporation, some statutes require that a specific proportion of the stock—usually a minimum amount—be subscribed, and some require that a certain portion of that stock subscribed for be actually paid in. Other statutes require that the articles state the amount of paid-in capital with which the corporation will begin business. The corporation is forbidden to begin business until the amount specified is paid. Such requirements are essential and should be complied with.

Any attempt to acquire corporate life and functions by a pretentious or evasive compliance with the statute as to issue of, or payment for, stock, no matter what the papers of the corporation say upon their face, legally are considered fraudulent. A substantial compliance with the requirements is sufficient. A majority of the states have simplified the statutes and reduced the formal requirements for incorporation.

De Jure and De Facto Corporations

A *"de jure"* corporation is one which has been regularly created in compliance with all requirements, has the legal sanction and authority of the state behind it. It is, therefore, invulnerable to attack or legal question. You will have this kind of corporation when you follow the statutes. An association which has not complied with the statutory requirements, but which has actually operated as a corporation and held itself out to the general public as a corporation, is called a corporation *"de facto."* That is, this type of corporation exists from the fact of its acting as such, though not in law or rightfully a corporation. It is an apparent corporation organization where the individual members claim it is a valid corporation, and it is acting as such, without the authoritative sanction of the law. It is an organization with color of law (as though it had followed the law), exercising corporate rights and franchises, and that status may not be challenged by anyone except the sovereign. A corporation de facto is, in short, a corporation in fact.

As a general rule, a corporation de facto exists when (1) there has been an attempt to comply with the statutory requirements, but some irregularity or defect in compliance has occurred, (2) the organization holds itself out to the public as a legal corporation, and (3) the de facto organization functions and operates as though it were

55

actually a legal corporation. The reason for this rule is that if rights and franchises have been infringed upon, they are the rights and franchises of the state. Until the state questions the validity of the de facto corporation, the public may treat those acting as possessing and exercising the corporate powers as doing so legally. The rule is in the interest of the public and is essential to the validity of business transactions with corporations. However, it is not recommended that anyone attempt to operate a legitimate business as de facto.

Status and Liability of Members

Ordinarily, according to law, persons who combine their capital in a business venture are liable as partners unless they are protected by incorporation. The decisive question in determining personal liability is whether what has been done toward incorporation and organization is sufficient to constitute a corporation. If it is, then the individuals are not personally liable. Therefore, it is important for incorporators to fulfill the requirements of a valid corporation. This emphasizes the importance of making sure you do not have a de facto corporation.

4

Corporate Existence and Franchises

Promoters and Promotion of Corporations

A promoter is a person who initiates the incorporation and organization of a corporation, procures for it the rights and capital by which to carry out the purposes set forth in its charter, and establishes it as able to do business. He or she brings together the persons interested in the enterprise, aids in acquiring subscriptions, and sets in motion the machinery which leads to the corporation itself. Signing and verifying articles of incorporation and subscribing for stock in the proposed company does not necessarily make one a promoter; neither does forming your own corporation.

Every person acting by whatever name in the forming and establishing of a corporation at any period prior to the company's becoming fully incorporated is considered, in law, as occupying a fiduciary relationship (position of trust) toward the corporation. A promoter stands in a fiduciary relation to both the corporation as a separate, legal entity and the individual stockholders and is bound to exercise good faith in all dealings with them.

57

Promoters must fully disclose all essential facts touching their relationship with the corporation, stockholders, officers, directors, or any other parties.

The fiduciary position of promoters requires that all of their dealings be open and fair. They will not be allowed to benefit by any secret profit or advantage which may be gained at the expense of the corporation or its members. However, this relationship does not prevent the promoters from fairly and openly doing business with the corporation at a profit. Any payment or reward offered to promoters for their services must be with a full disclosure of the facts. And a custom of promoters to divide secretly among themselves a certain portion of the stock of the corporation is fraudulent.

Until articles of incorporation have been filed and approved or other essential steps are taken to bring a corporation into legal existence, a corporation has no being, franchise, or faculties. Its promoters or those bringing it into existence are in no sense identical with the corporation. They do not represent it in any relation of agency and do not have any authority to enter into preliminary contracts binding upon the corporation. It follows that a corporation cannot, before its organization, have agents, contract for itself, or be contracted with. It is, therefore, not legally liable or responsible for any contract which a promoter attempts to make prior to its organization. A promoter's contract does not, by the incorporation of the contemplated company, become the contract of the corporation. This demonstrates the importance of your completing all steps necessary for incorporation before you begin operating a business as a corporation.

Courts of equity refuse to enforce a contract against a corporation made on its behalf by promoters, agents, or others unless there appears to be some sound reason for demanding its enforcement. It is, of course, perfectly proper and legal after incorporation, to assume voluntarily those contracts made by promoters or agents. In these situations the corporation may sue upon the contract to enforce it or recover for its breach.

A promoter who makes a contract for the benefit of the corporation, before incorporation, is personally liable on it and incurs personal liability. It frequently happens that a promoter conducts the ordinary affairs of the business as a corporation before legal incorporation. In such a case, the promoter becomes personally liable on business contracts. You are cautioned to complete all legal requirements for incorporation before engaging in any business activities in the corporate name.

Corporate Name and Seal

A name is necessary to the very existence of a corporation. Each corporation must have a name by which it can be identified, function, and operate in the conduct of any legal acts or activities. The name of a corporation designates the corporation in the same manner as the name of an individual. The right to use its corporate name is one of the legal attributes of incorporation and constitutes a franchise or a privilege granted by the state. The presence or absence in a trade name of the word "company," in and of itself, has no direct bearing on the issue as to whether the association is a corporation, partnership, or other entity.

Most statutes prohibit a private corporation from using the words "bank," "insurance," 'trust," and other names which may mislead the public. A corporation may adopt any name it desires, subject to the qualification that it cannot adopt or use a name already used by another. Corporations and unincorporated associations, may have a property right in their names. A corporation cannot adopt a name so similar to that of another corporation, association, or firm as would result in confusion or deception. It may not use its name for the purposes of pirating the business of a competitor. A corporation cannot adopt the name of an individual where it appears that the use of such name would lead to confusion, deception to the public, or defraud others operating a business under the same name, even though the name was taken from the names of principal stockholders, promoters, or incorporators.

A corporation may use and adopt any seal or mark as

its official corporate seal. Under former common law rules a corporate seal was essential for valid contracts, however, this is no longer required as a matter of law. In all business transactions and legal relationships where a natural person will be legally bound without a seal, a corporation will also be bound. For this reason it is not necessary to obtain a corporate seal, though it is usually one of the items in the corporate kit. Even though the seal is not legally necessary, the presence of the corporate seal establishes, on its face, that the instrument to which it is affixed is the act of the corporation.

Bylaws

The bylaws of a corporation govern it. They prescribe the relationship of the rights and duties of the members to the internal government of the corporation; establish the procedures, practices, and policies of the business operation; approve the rules for the management of the corporate affairs; and establish the rights and duties existing among the members. Bylaws are self-imposed rules to regulate the manner in which the corporation will function. They include all self-made regulations of a corporation, but generally do not bind or affect the rights of third persons. Until repealed, the bylaws are continuing rules for the government of the corporation and its officers, their function being to regulate the transaction of the incidental business of the corporation.

Bylaws differ from *corporate resolutions* in that a resolution applies to a single act of the corporation while the bylaws govern only with reference to the rules which the directors and officers may pass for their government. Bylaws are valid if they are reasonable and calculated to carry into effect the objectives of the corporation. They cannot be in conflict with the general policy of the state and federal laws.

Records and Reports

The records of a corporation include its articles of incorporation and bylaws, the minutes of its meetings, the stock books, the books containing the account of its official activities, and the written evidence of its contracts and business transactions. They are the property of the corporation, not of the officers or employees. Most state statutes require the keeping of such books and records. Another requirement is that corporations make periodic statements or reports to the state agency regulating corporations.

Stockholders have a right to inspect the books and records of a corporation, subject to reasonable company regulations. Inconvenience to the business from an inspection of its books is no ground for a denial of the stockholder's right to examine the records. A stock- holder's right cannot be defeated by a corporation's offer to purchase his shares of stock. Moreover, an offer to furnish extracts or copies from the books or to furnish annual reports will not satisfy a demand for inspection of the original records. It is easy to see that a stockholder's lawsuit or other demands of shareholders for examination of corporate books and records could result in considerable expense, inconvenience, and disruption of the business operations of a corporation. In an attempt to resolve this problem, the courts, while recognizing the fundamental right of the stockholder to examine the books and records, have placed certain restrictions upon the exercise of those rights. One of the most important of these qualifications is that before the right of inspection will be granted over the corporation's objection, an inquiry by the court will be made into the applicant's motives.

Capital and Capital Stock

There is a difference between capital and capital stock. The *capital stock* of a corporation is the amount of money, property, or other means authorized by its articles of incorporation and contributed, or agreed to be contributed, by the shareholders as the financial basis for the operation of the business. These contributions are usually received from the capital investment of the shareholders or through the declaration of stock dividends.

Capital is sometimes used broadly to indicate the entire assets of the corporation, regardless of their source, which is utilized for the conduct of the corporate business and for the purpose of making gains and profits. In this sense the capital belongs to the corporation, and capital stock, when issued, belongs to the stockholders. Capital may be either real or personal property, but capital stock is always personal property. The terms are frequently used interchangeably, but it is important to note the difference.

Classes of Stock

A *share of stock* is a unit of interest in a corporation. Even though ownership of stock does not confer title to any of the property of the corporation, it legally entitles the shareholder to an equivalent part of the property, or its proceeds, when distributed. Each share represents a distinct and undivided share or interest in the common property of the corporation. Shares of stock constitute property distinct from the capital or tangible property of the corporation and belong to different owners. The capital is the property of the corporation. The shares of stock are the property of the several shareholders. You should not treat corporate property and assets as yours even though you may own all, or substantially all, of the stock of the corporation.

Common stock is the class of stock ordinarily issued without extraordinary rights or privileges, and which, in the absence of other cases of stock having superior rights, represents the complete interest in the corporation. *Pre-ferred stock* has different characteristics from, and is entitled to certain preferences over, common stock. What distinguishes preferred stock is that it is entitled to a priority over other stock in the distribution of profits, being ordinarily entitled to dividends of a definite percentage or amount. Sometimes this right to a prior dividend is the only preference which is given to such stock. Upon dissolution of the corporation preferred stockholders may, by agreement, be given a preference over common stockholders in the distribution of the capital assets of a corporation. Preferred stock is sometimes thought of as an investment rather than participating ownership of a business.

Par value stock has imprinted upon its face a dollar value. The par value of a share is simply an amount fixed as the nominal value of the interest so specified. This amount likewise indicates the sum of money or value of property or services which a subscriber is represented as having contributed to the corporation in exchange for such share in its ownership. Par value and actual value of issued stock are not necessarily the same. Par value stock is also to be distinguished from *non par stock*, which is simply stock without any nominal or par value.

The usual practice for a small corporation is to issue only common stock. It is also recommended that you authorize the issuance of the maximum number of shares for the minimum filing fee, but that you issue only a limited number of shares in the beginning.

Subscriptions and Purchase
of Shares from the Corporation

Subscribers of stock are those who agree to take and pay for shares of the capital stock; they agree with each other to pay the par value of the stock. Shares of stock are personal property, therefore most of the principles governing rights and liabilities of the parties to a contract are applicable to sales of shares of stock. You should not make any sale of stock to the general public without complying with any applicable securities regulations or making sure the transaction is exempt.

Status, Rights, and Duties of Stockholders or Members

Ordinarily, neither the general statutes nor the articles of incorporation impose any qualification as to who may be stockholders. A corporation is a legal entity distinct from the body of its stockholders, and it represents its stockholders in all matters within the scope of its powers. A stockholder does not stand in any fiduciary relation to the directors of the corporation; rather, the directors and officers of a corporation occupy a fiduciary or quasi-fiduciary relation (resembling a position of trust) to the corporation and its stockholders. One remains a stockholder in a corporation until he transfers his shares to another person or until his status is terminated by the forfeiture of his stock. Strictly speaking, a stockholder cannot resign from a corporation.

A corporation organized for profit has no power to expel a member or declare a forfeiture of his stock, even for nonpayment of its assessments. A corporation may not adopt bylaws imposing the forfeiture of stock or of other corporate interest as a penalty for its breach, unless the power to pass such bylaws is expressly granted by the articles of incorporation. Moreover, any power given to forfeit stock must be strictly construed. If any restrictions or limitations imposed by the articles of incorporation have been disregarded, the alleged act of forfeiture will be declared invalid. A stockholder has a right to contract with a corporation as a stranger, provided the contract is in good faith.

Meetings of Stockholders or Members

Generally, the purpose of stockholder's meetings is to elect directors and transact other business calling for, or requiring, the action or consent of the stockholders. For example, meetings are called for amendment of the articles of incorporation, sale or mortgage of the corporate assets, consolidation and merger, or other relevant business. Individual stockholders are bound by the action of the majority attending corporate meetings. Due notice of meetings is given. Most small corporations have few stockholders' meetings because the control is usually in one or two people and regular, formal meetings of stockholders are of little value.

Under some statutes, at least one meeting of stockholders must be held annually and, whether or not the statute states so specifically, this requirement is usually included in the bylaws. The matter of giving notice of stockholder's meetings is now generally regulated by statutes which usually require notice to be given of the time and place of the regular, annual meeting as well as of special meetings.

Stockholders' Liabilities to Creditors

In the absence of a charter, generally, constitutional, or statutory provisions to the contrary, stockholders are not liable, for any of the obligations of a corporation, whatever their character and in whatever manner incurred. The corporation is an entity distinct from its members, and, therefore, its debts are not the debts of its members. It is held that stockholders, unless they participate, are not liable for the wrongful acts of corporate agents and employees. The rule is not ordinarily affected by the fact that one person owns all or most of the stock in the corporation.

Powers and Functions of Corporations

A corporation owes its existence to the will of the

state. An individual has an absolute right to use, enjoy, and dispose of all his acquisitions, without any control except by the laws of the land. The individual may perform all acts and make all contracts which are not, in the eye of the law, inconsistent with the welfare of society. However, the civil rights of a corporation are very different. A corporation has only those powers which are expressly granted in its articles of incorporation or in the statutes under which it is created. The decision of what business may be carried on by a corporation must be referred to its articles of incorporation. Without this stated power to carry on a particular business, it does not exist. It is important that you specify powers and purposes in the articles of incorporation that will generally include all acts authorized by law.

Directors, Officers, and Employees

All corporations must act and contract by means of its officers, agents, and employees. They may either hold corporate offices or be agents appointed by the appropriate officials in the regular course of the corporate business. Corporations have the power to appoint agents with full power and authority to do all things necessary and proper to enter into contracts with other corporations, individuals, or other business entities.

Directors of corporations are usually stockholders. However, it is generally not necessary to be a stockholder to be eligible as a director or trustee. The board of directors represents the impersonal corporate body, and the directors are the executive representatives of the corporation. The directors are not ordinary agents in the immediate control of the stockholders. The powers of boards of directors are, in a very important sense, original and undelegated. The stockholders do not confer, nor can they revoke, those powers or create a sterilized board of directors. The law imposes the business management of a corporation on its directors, and a corporation can act only through its directors. This is entirely consistent with the principle that the corporate entity is separate and distinct from the individual owner or owners. The stockholders do not have the general management and control of the affairs of the corporation, and they are deemed to have consented to the management and control of the corporate business by the board of directors.

The directors are authorized to transact and have the power to do whatever they, as individuals, could do if the business were theirs. A usual practice within the power of the board of directors is to appoint and authorize a committee to act for the corporation in specific or particular matters. The board may grant to this committee all authority necessary to conduct the ordinary business of the corporation.

The legal principles regarding the powers and authority of an *officer* or agent of a corporation are basically the same as those applicable to any agent. The authority of a corporate officer, agent, or employee may be actual in the sense that it is specifically given, or it may be implied in the sense that the agent holds himself out as having authority to act.

Rights and Liabilities between
Corporation and Third Persons

As a general rule, a corporation is bound by the acts of its officers or agents who are acting within the scope of their express, implied, or apparent authority. It is not always easy to determine when an agent exceeds his authority. A corporation is not bound by acts done, or declarations made, by an officer or agent who does this. For a corporation to be bound by the acts of its officers, agents, or employees, it must be established that the corporation knew of the acts which indicated implied or apparent authority to third persons.

Dissolution

Corporations are easy to create, and they are easy to terminate or dissolve. The state gives a corporation its existence and status as an entity, and it cannot be terminated except by some act of the sovereign power by which it was created. The courts of another state do not have the power to dissolve a corporation created by the laws of your state. In the event a corporation fails to pay franchise taxes or other taxes or assessments made by the state, it may be automatically dissolved by the state. This is a forfeiture of the grant of corporate existence by failure to comply with the statutory requirements. In this instance, the secretary of state merely declares a forfeiture of the grant, and declares the corporation dissolved and at an end. By following the statute relating to dissolution of corporations, you may voluntarily dissolve your corporation. Essentially, this involves the completion of another form you file with the secretary of state in which the corporation is voluntarily dissolved and terminated.

Special Tax Tips

Sub Chapter S Election

If you have no more than 15 stockholders, you will certainly wish to consider whether to adopt an option under the tax code to have profits of the corporation flow through to stockholders to be taxed individually rather than at corporate tax rates. You should review the booklets and easy to follow instructions which are available at any Internal Revenue Office or the Post Office.

You must file Form 2553, "Election by a Small Business Corporation," to make the election. The rules for eligibility as stated on Form 2553 are as follows:

The corporation may make the election only if it meets all six of the following requirements:

1. It is a domestic corporation;
2. It has no more than 15 shareholders (a husband and

wife and their estates shall be treated as one shareholder);
3. It has only individuals, estates, or certain trusts as
shareholders;
4. It has no nonresident alien shareholders;
5. It has only one class of stock;
6. It is not a member of an affiliated group of corporations as defined in section 1504 of the Internal Revenue
Code.

For taxable years beginning after December 31, 1978, this form can be filed (1) any time during the preceding taxable year, or (2) any time during the first 75 days of the tax year.

An election by a small business corporation shall terminate if a new shareholder (any person who was not a shareholder on the day on which the election was made) becomes a shareholder in such corporation and affirma-tively refuses to consent to the election on or before the 60th day after the day on which the new shareholder acquires the stock.

Most small business owners prefer to elect to have Sub Chapter S corporations. However, there are long range tax aspects that you may wish to discuss with your accountant.

Section 1244 Stock

When you form a corporation you should issue "Sec-tion 1244 Stock." Under Section 1244 of the Internal Revenue Code you are permitted, under certain circumstances, to take ordinary tax loss treatment for certain stock issues. It is a very simple matter to comply with the requirements of Section 1244 for issuing your corporate stock.

When you comply with the simple requirements of the Code, a loss on a sale, exchange, or worthlessness of the Section 1244 stock is fully deductible as an ordinary loss rather than as a capital loss. Any amount not absorbed in the year sustained becomes a part of the stockholder's net operating loss carryback and carryover.

The rule applies only to an individual who must be the original buyer, either directly or through a partnership. The maximum allowable as an ordinary loss in one tax year is $50,000. On a joint return, it is $100,000 whether the stock is owned by one or both spouses. Any excess loss is subject to capital loss limitations.

Only common stock, voting or nonvoting, of a domestic corporation qualifies as Section 1244 stock. The stock must be issued for money or other property, but not for stock or securities. For purposes of the Code requirements, a corporation will be treated as a small business corporation if the aggregate amount of money and other property received by the corporation for stock, as a contribution to capital, and as paid in surplus, as of the time the stock is issued, does not exceed $1,000,000. The value of the other property is its adjusted basis to the corporation for figuring gain, reduced by any liability which the property is subject to, or was assumed by the corporation.

The ordinary loss treatment of Section 1244 stock applies only if, for the five tax years of the corporation ending before the loss, less than 50 percent of its gross receipts was from investment sources such as interest, dividends, rents, royalties, and stock or security gains. But this limitation does not apply if deductions, excluding those for operating loss, partially tax free interest, and dividends received, exceed gross income. However, the corporation must be an operating company.

Before the Revenue Act of 1978 it was necessary to have a written plan in the records of the corporation to qualify as Section 1244 stock, however, the 1978 Act eliminated this requirement. It is still necessary to have adequate records to establish compliance with the Code requirements. These corporate records should include proper records reflecting the following information:

1. The person to whom the stock was issued, stock certificates, dates of issue, amount and type of consideration received from each shareholder, including shareholder's basis and value of property;

2. Amount of money and the corporation's basis of property received for its stock as a contribution to capital, and as paid in surplus;

3. Equity capital on date of adoption of plan; and

4. Stock dividends and reorganizations, if any.

Minutes of the corporation board of directors can

qualify as a plan if they contain all of these required elements. Taxpayers claiming deductions must file a statement with his or her return showing the address of the corporation, how the stock was acquired and the nature and amount of the consideration paid, including the type, value and basis of property given in a nontaxable exchange. Each taxpayer should also keep records to distinguish the Section 1244 stock from other stock owned in the same corporation.

There are a number of other tax advantages to incorporating your business. It is recommended that you confer with your accountant or tax lawyer for further details as they become appropriate.

5

The Foreign Corporation:
Doing Business in Other States

We have already discussed the economic and legal hazards among other disadvantages of your forming a corporation in a "foreign" forum—another state or country—to operate business activities in your own state. The additional expenses—very substantial in most cases—and the potential exposure to personal as well as the legal liabilities of your corporation are all totally unnecessary. Moreover, you would be unduly complicating the very simple procedure of incorporation.

There are many problems you should know about in operating as a foreign corporation, whether it is a foreign corporation doing business in your state or your domestic corporation doing business in another state. These include:

1. statutory qualifications procedures and requirements along with the attendant expenses,
2. civil and criminal penalties for failure to comply,
3. potential fines and personal liabilities,
4. exposure to service of process in another state,

5. potential taxation hazards, and others.

After reviewing these items if you still want a foreign corporation I strongly recommend you get good legal advice from a competent lawyer. If you have some "secret" activities or clandestine operations which impel you to foreign forum shopping, I would suggest Wyoming as the best state "shop" at this time, but better still, if you must go, go to the "islands." If you go "foreign," go all the way.

We will confine the following discussions to the legal principles of law involved in a foreign corporation "qualifying" in states where it does business, the exposure to service of process in other states, the exposure to taxation in other states, and the exposure to personal liability and criminal penalties of officers, directors, or agents who fail to comply with statutory qualification procedures by foreign corporations.

But remember: This is only the "foreign corporation" gambit. If you form your corporation in your own state and are not "doing business" in some other state or country you don't have to bother about these sticky questions.

What Is "Doing Business" in Another State?

All corporate directors, officers, agents, and employees should know the ever present potential liabilities and penalties of doing business in another state without qualification in that state. It doesn't matter whether your corporation is "doing business" in another state or a foreign corporation does business with you, or your corporation, in your state. It works both ways. If you slip up, it may be costly to you; if the other guy slips up in your state you may have a great advantage over him in any dispute or lawsuit. In all events it is vital to know about it if you are to live up to the responsibilities imposed by the law on corporate officials.

A corporation is, for most purposes, a citizen of the state of incorporation. Although a corporation has the capacity to exercise its powers in other states, it has no inherent right to exist or do business there without first getting permission from the state. Each state has a legitimate purpose and motive in exercising the power to exclude or restrict foreign corporations based on public policy, and the protection of its residents. But this general rule is subject to certain qualifications. The Interstate Commerce Clause, the Due Process Clause, the Equal Privileges and Immunities Clause, and the Equal Protection of the Laws Clauses of the United States Constitution grants certain fundamental rights to "citizens" and "persons" which cannot be abridged by the several states.

When a corporation does business outside of the state in which it is organized, it may be required to "qualify." That is, it must obtain a certificate of authority and appoint a resident agent upon whom process may be served, and take any other steps required by statutes. The corporation laws of all of the states require qualification of foreign corporations. Although there is no comprehensive definition of the term "doing business" that will answer all questions that may arise, it is important for you to know about the meaning of the phrase "doing business" as that term is used by the courts.

In all states, unqualified foreign corporations doing intrastate business are denied access to the courts and may therefore be unable to enforce contracts or collect debts in the state. Some foreign corporations, because of the potential liability, take precautions by qualifying even when there is doubt as to whether or not they are required to do so. Some corporate officials are unaware of the extent to which their corporations may be doing business in another state. Failure to qualify may subject a foreign corporation to fines. In several states, directors, officers, and agents of such corporations may be fined or even imprisoned; or may be held personally liable on contracts entered into in the state by the corporation.

The concept of "doing business" in a foreign state generally arises in three contexts: (1) qualification, (2) service of process (Long Arm Statutes), and (3) taxation.

One court, in describing the situation, stated that:

. . . the three general types of "doing business" have reference to the question before the court, i.e., whether the foreign corporation is subject to the state's taxing jurisdiction, whether it is subject to the process of the court

80

within the state and whether or not it has subjected itself to the regulatory or qualification statutes of the state depend to a greater or less extent on the amount of activity of the corporation within the state. . . . This much seems to be clear that the greatest amount of business activity is required to subject a corporation to the state's statutory qualification requirements. [Filmakers Releasing Organ v. Realart, 374 S.W. 2d 335]

Recent decisions of the United States Supreme Court and the language of the state statutes, have eroded the struggle over the term "doing business" to the point where the slightest activity can subject your corporation to the jurisdiction of the foreign state. The starting point in understanding the laws relative to the doing business concept is, first, the language of the state statutes in question; second, the constitutional limitations imposed by the federal constitution; and, third, the interpretations placed on thé statutes by the court. One classic statement is:

It is established by well considered general authorities that a foreign corporation is doing, transacting, carrying on, or engaging in business within a state when it transacts some substantial part of its ordinary business therein. [Royal Insurance Co. v. All States Theatres, 6 So 2d 494 (Ala 1942)]

"Doing business" is really not subject to a precise definition, but depends upon the particular facts and circumstances of each case. It is almost like saying it is a "jury question." It is a fact issue to be decided in each case on the evidence. The cumulative facts, the totality of the corporate activities, are the controlling criteria upon which the court decisions are based.

Frequently courts are presented with the question of the necessity of qualifying when an out-of-state corporation files a lawsuit against a local party who raises as a defense the assertion that the foreign corporation failed to qualify under the state statutes and therefore cannot, under the statute, have access to the courts of the state. The court then must determine whether the unlicensed foreign corporation was in fact doing business in the state in violation of the statute.

This can be a shocking, embarrassing, and expensive experience for corporate officers. If your corporation is doing business in another state, if it might later be doing business in another state, or if you don't know whether it is doing business in another state, for any of the purposes mentioned above, you should take a look at the statutes of the states in question and take whatever steps may be necessary to comply with the laws.

Qualification

"Qualification" is easier to define. It is the process by which a foreign corporation signifies its presence in the state and by which it submits itself to the laws and conditions of admission to do business in the state as legally prescribed. This process generally consists of the filing of the documents specified by the statutes and state regula-

82

tions which usually includes an application for admission, the designation of an agent upon whom service of process may be made, and the payment of an admission fee. It is about the same as filing the papers to form your corporation in your own state. And it is just as simple; you don't need a lawyer to do it.

Technically, the "qualification" means the fulfilling of any act required by the state statute which is requisite to have the foreign corporation officially submit itself to the state's jurisdiction. Penalties are imposed for lack of proper compliance. Qualification may also include establishing the principal place of business in the state, keeping books in the state, and filing statements of financial condition. Again, these are much like the requirements of your own state where you incorporated. There are certain limitations on the scope of these statutes imposed by the interstate commerce clause and the due process clause of the federal constitution, but these have almost been taken away in a flood of judicial decisions favorable to "governmental control" of business operations.

The question is frequently presented as to just what activities in another state constitutes doing business so as to require corporation compliance with the qualification statutes. Generally more business activity is required to generate the necessity for qualification than for other purposes such as taxation, process, and regulation.

A corporation which is engaged exclusively in interstate commerce—and not intrastate business need not qualify. This would be an undue burden on commerce within the meaning of the Interstate Commerce Clause of the federal constitution.

Many of the state statutes are explicit about what activities do, or do not, constitute "doing business" and just what activities will require a foreign corporation to qualify in the state. The necessity of qualification and the commerce clause of the U.S. Constitution are inextricably intertwined. Qualification statutes, by their nature, are regulatory and cannot be imposed on corporations engaged exclusively in interstate commerce without denying such corporations the protection afforded interstate commerce by the Commerce Clause. The immunity of corporations engaged exclusively in interstate commerce from such regulatory statutes was restated by the U.S. Supreme Court in Eli Lilly and Company v. Sav-On Drugs, Inc., 366 U.S. 276 (1961):

> It is well established that New Jersey cannot require Lilly to get a certificate of authority to do business in the State if its participation in this trade is limited to its wholly interstate sales to New Jersey wholesalers.[278]
> . . . it is equally well settled that if Lilly is engaged in *intrastate* as well as *interstate* aspects of the New Jersey drug business, the State can require it to get a certificate of authority to do business. [279]

Service of Process: Long Arm Statutes

Service of process on an unlicensed foreign corporation turns on the "contacts" with the state and on "traditional notions of fair play and substantial justice." The legal arguments generated by the legal issue as to whether the courts of one state can exercise *in personam jurisdiction* over persons residing in another state or a foreign corporation has been one of the most challenging, changing, and momentous issues in our legal system. Can a person living in Los Angeles, for example, sue a person who lives in Miami, Florida, in the Superior Court in Los Angeles thereby requiring him to "go to court" in California? If so, under what circumstances? Or can a resident of Plains, Georgia, sue a resident of Fairbanks, Alaska, in the local courts of Georgia? Can your corporation get sued in the courts of New York? Or Wyoming? The legality, constitutionality, and the fairness of these situations and others are extremely important to you and your corporation.

Three of the leading U.S. Supreme Court cases on this issue are International Shoe Co. v. Washington, 326 U.S. 310 (1945); McGee v. International Life Insurance Co., 355 U.S. 220 (1957); and Hanson v. Denckla, 357 U.S. 235 (1958). The courts have generally stated the rules established by the U.S. Supreme Court on the issues as follows:

Rule 1. The nonresident defendant must do some act or

consummate some transaction within the forum. It is not necessary that the defendant's agent be physically within the forum, for this act or transaction may be by mail only. A single event will suffice if its effects within the state are substantial enough to qualify under Rule Three.

Rule 2. The cause of action must be one which arises out of, or results from, the activities of the defendant within the forum. It is conceivable that the actual cause of action might come to fruition in another state, but because of the activities of defendant in the forum state there would still be "substantial minimum contact."

Rule 3. Having established by Rules One and Two a minimum contact between the defendant and the state, the assumption of jurisdiction based upon such contact must be consonant with the due process tenants of "fair play" and "substantial justice." If this test is fulfilled, there exists a "substantial minimum contact" between the forum and the defendant. The reasonableness of subjecting the defendant to jurisdiction under this rule is frequently tested by standards analogous to those of forum non conveniens.

Taxation

In 1959 the Congress enacted 15 U.S.C. 381, a statute which limited to some extent the taxing powers of the states. Essentially the statute prohibits states and political subdivisions from imposing a net income tax on income derived within the state from interstate commerce where the activities of the taxpayer in the state are limited to the solicitation of orders.

The purpose of the statute was to clarify certain aspects of the intent of the Interstate Commerce Clause of the U.S. Constitution. It was stated by one court that:

> ... "solicitation" should be limited to those generally accepted or customary acts in the industry which lead to the placing of orders, not those who follow as a natural result of the transaction, such as collections, servicing complaints, technical assistance and training. [Olympia Brewing Co. v. Department of Revenue, 50 TR 99, 110 (1972)]

In most cases one of the underlying questions is whether the activities of the foreign corporation are sufficient to constitute the doing of *intrastate* business so as to remove the corporation from the protection of the Interstate Commerce Clause. Many court decisions have weighed the significance, alone and cumulatively, of various business activities. Some activities have been universally held to constitute "doing business," such as maintaining a stock of goods in a state from which deliveries are regularly made to customers in that state. Other activities, standing alone, have been held to fall short of doing business. For example, the mere solicitation of orders, or the maintenance of an office in furtherance of the interstate activities of the corporation.

The right of a state to tax the activities of a foreign corporation is limited by Article I, Section 8 of the U.S. Constitution which says that, "The Congress shall have power . . . to regulate Commerce . . . among the several states." Thus, the constitution doesn't bar a state from taxing a foreign corporation for the privilege of doing *intrastate* business, nor from taxing the income of a foreign corporation derived from its *intrastate* business, even though it may also be doing an interstate business. But, can a state tax the exclusively *interstate* activities of a foreign corporation? The Federal Statute, 15 U.S.C. 381, and court cases say no—but there are many qualifications and limitations to the rule.

The most recent, leading case on this issue is National Geographic Society v. California Board of Equalization, 97 S. Ct 1386 (1977) in which it was held that California's imposition of a use tax collection liability on the Society's mail order operation does not violate the Due Process Clause of the Fourteenth Amendment or the Commerce Clause since the Society's continuous presence in California in the two offices provides a sufficient nexus between the Society and the State to justify imposition of the use tax collection liability as applied to the Society. (For other cases, look up in your local law library: Complete Auto Transit, Inc. v. Brady, 97 S. Ct 1076 (1977); Piper v. Chris-Craft Industries, Inc., 97 S. Ct 926 (1977); and Santa Fe Industries, Inc. v. Green, 97 S. Ct 1292 (1977).)

Finally, you can form your corporation (or several corporations) in your own state and operate a business there. You can do it yourself without a lawyer. But if you organize a "foreign corporation" or do business in a foreign state or country make sure you investigate all of the potential dangers involved.

Appendix A

Statement of Corporate Purposes in Articles of Incorporation

General or Blanket Purpose Clauses

1. To manufacture, purchase, or otherwise acquire, own, mortgage, pledge, sell, assign, and transfer, or otherwise dispose of, to invest, trade, deal in and deal with, goods, wares, and merchandise and real and personal property of every class and description.

2. To engage in any commercial, industrial, and agricultural enterprise calculated or designed to be profitable to this corporation and in conformity with the laws of the states in which business is transacted;

To generally engage in, do, and perform, any enterprises, act, or vocation that a natural person might or could do or perform;

To engage in the manufacture, sale, purchase, importing, and exporting of merchandise and personal property of all manner and description, to act as agents for the purchase, sale, and handling of goods, wares, and merchandise of any and all types and descriptions for the account of the corporation or as factor, agent, procurer, or otherwise for or on behalf of another.

3. To manufacture, produce, purchase, or otherwise acquire, sell, or otherwise dispose of, import, export, distribute, deal in and with, whether as principal or agent, goods, wares, merchandise, and materials of every kind and description, whether now known or hereafter to be discovered or invented.

4. The purposes for which the corporation is formed are:

a. To engage primarily in the specific business of selling, buying, manufacturing, marketing, and distributing real and personal property of every kind and description.

b. To engage generally in the business of retail and wholesale selling, advertising, and marketing of services of every kind and description.

c. To engage in any business, related or unrelated to those described in clauses a and b of this Article, from time to time authorized or approved by the board of directors of this corporation or carry on any other trade or business which can, in the opinion of the board of directors of the company, be advantageously carried on in connection with or auxiliary to those described in clauses a and b of this Article, and to do all such things as are incidental or conducive to the attainment of the above objects or any of them.

d. To become a member of any partnership or joint

venture and to enter into any lawful arrangement for sharing profits and/or losses in any transaction or transactions, and to promote and organize other corporations.

e. To do business anywhere in the world.

f. To have and to exercise all rights and powers that are now or may hereafter be granted to a corporation by law.

g. To have and to exercise all rights and powers that are now or may hereafter be granted to a corporation by law.

h. To acquire, hold, lease, encumber, convey, or otherwise dispose of real and personal property within or without the state, and take real and personal property by will, gift, or bequest.

i. To assume any obligations, enter into any contracts, or do any acts incidental to the transaction of its business or to the issue or sale of its securities, or expedient for the attainment of its obligations by mortgage or otherwise.

j. To borrow money and issue bonds, debentures, notes and evidences of indebtedness, and secure the payment of performance of its obligations by mortgage or otherwise.

k. To acquire, subscribe for, hold, own, pledge, and otherwise dispose of and represent shares of stock, bonds, and securities of any other corporation, domestic or

91

foreign.

l. To purchase or otherwise acquire its own bonds, debentures, or other evidences of its indebtedness or obligation, and, subject to the provisions of the corporation laws of the state of incorporation, purchase or otherwise acquire its own shares.

m. Subject to the provisions of these Articles, to redeem shares thereby made subject to redemption.

n. To make donations for the public welfare or for charitable, scientific, or education purposes.

o. To sue and be sued in any court.

p. To adopt, use, and at will, alter a corporate seal, but failure to affix a seal shall not affect the validity of any instrument.

q. To make bylaws.

r. To appoint such subordinate officers or agents as its business may require, and to allow them suitable compensation.

The foregoing shall be construed as objects, purposes, and powers, and the enumeration thereof shall not be held to limit or restrict in any manner the powers now or hereafter conferred on this corporation by the laws of the state of incorporation or any state within which business may be carried on.

The objects, purposes, and powers specified herein shall, except as otherwise expressed, be in no way limited or restricted by reference to or inference from the terms of any purposes, and powers specified in each of the clauses or paragraphs of these Articles of Incorporation shall be regarded as independent objects, purposes, or powers.

The corporation may in its bylaws confer powers, not in conflict with law, upon its directors in addition to the foregoing and in addition to the powers and authorities expressly conferred upon them by statute.

Additional Clauses for Specific Businesses

Agency and Business Promotion

To transact the business of advertising, promoting, and developing the business of other corporations, partnerships, or individuals for hire, or upon commission, or otherwise, by and through the means of preparing advertising for other corporations, partnerships, or individuals, and of advertising the business, commodities, or other property, real, personal, or mixed, of other corporations, partnerships, or individuals in newspapers, books, booklets, prospectuses, magazines, circulars, pamphlets, or other similar literature and advertising media.

Art and Artists Supplies Dealer

To carry on the business of holders of exhibitions and dealers in pictures, and makers and sellers of picture frames, artists' colors, oils, paints, paint brushes, and other instruments, articles, and ingredients relating to any such business.

Bookstore

To conduct and carry on in all of its branches and business of buying, selling, and dealing in and with books of any and all kinds, whether new or old, and manuscripts, prints, engravings, lithographs, pamphlets, writings, publications, stationery, and similar goods or merchandise; to conduct the business of an agency in all of its branches for any and all of the goods or merchandise; to acquire and carry on a selling agency or agencies for the sale of any and all merchandise pertaining or relating to books, manuscripts, prints, engravings, lithographs, pamphlets, writings, and similar goods or merchandise; to deal in and with goods, wares, and merchandise and personal property of every and any sort, nature, or description.

Farm Ownership and Farming

To purchase, own, improve, equip, operate, and manage farms and engage in any agricultural pursuit or undertaking.

Furniture Manufacture

To engage in the business of manufacturing wood and metal home and office furniture, cabinets, and other items, including their component parts and materials, of every nature and description.

Groceries

To merchandise, sell, offer for sale, and distribute at wholesale and retail, foods and foodstuffs of all kinds and descriptions, whether in bulk, package, bottle, or can, including beverages of all kinds and for all purposes, and to generally deal in groceries and grocery products suitable for public consumption.

Hardware Store

To engage in and operate a general hardware and mercantile business and to deal in, buy, and sell general hardware, electrical and gas appliances, housewares, toys, general merchandise including paints and painting supplies, but not excluding any other articles of merchandise sometimes dealt in by hardware establishments.

Marketing

To enter into contracts or agreements relating to sales campaigns and marketing and to the design, manufacture, operation, and use of tools and tooling of every kind, character, and description, including, without being limited to, mechanical, pneumatic, hydraulic, electrical, or artistic devices, articles, or designs with any and all persons, firms, corporations, or other legal entity, whether domestic or foreign.

Retail Stores

To establish, purchase, lease, as lessee, or otherwise acquire, to own, operate, and maintain, and to sell mortgage, lease or lessor, and otherwise dispose of retail stores or departments therein and to conduct a general merchandising business therein.

Appendix B

Names and Addresses of State Offices
Where New Corporation Papers Are Filed

Secretary of State
Montgomery, Alabama 36100

Commissioner of Commerce
Juneau, Alaska 99801

Secretary of State
Little Rock, Arkansas 72200

Secretary of State
Sacramento, California 95801

Secretary of State
Denver, Colorado 80202

Secretary of State
Hartford, Connecticut 06100

Secretary of State
Dover, Delaware 19901

Office of Superintendent of Corps
Washington, D.C. 20000

Secretary of State
Tallahassee, Florida 32301

Secretary of State
Atlanta, Georgia 30300

Director of Regulatory Agencies
P.O. Box 40
Honolulu, Hawaii 96800

Secretary of State
Boise, Idaho 83700

Secretary of State
Springfield, Illinois 62700

Secretary of State
Indianapolis, Indiana 46200

Secretary of State
Des Moines, Iowa 50300

Secretary of State
Topeka, Kansas 66600

Secretary of State
Frankfort, Kentucky 40601

Secretary of State
Baton Rouge, Louisiana 70800

Secretary of State
Augusta, Maine 04301

State Department of Assessment
and Taxation
Baltimore, Maryland 21200

Secretary of Commonwealth
Boston, Massachusetts 02100

Department of Commerce
Corporation Division
P.O. Drawer C
Lansing, Michigan 48904

Secretary of State
St. Paul, Minnesota 55100

Secretary of State
Jackson, Mississippi 39200

Secretary of State
Jefferson City, Missouri 65101

Secretary of State
Helena, Montana 59601

Secretary of State
Lincoln, Nebraska 68500

Secretary of State
Carson City, Nevada 89701

Secretary of State
Concord, New Hampshire 03300

Secretary of State
Trenton, New Jersey 08600

State Corporation Commission
Santa Fe, New Mexico 87501

Secretary of State
Albany, New York 12200

Secretary of State
Raleigh, North Carolina 27600

Secretary of State
Bismarck, North Dakota 58501

Secretary of State
Columbus, Ohio 43200

Secretary of State
Oklahoma City, Oklahoma 73100

Corporation Commissioner
Salem, Oregon 97301

Department of State
Harrisburg, Pennsylvania 17101

Secretary of State
Providence, Rhode Island 02900

Secretary of State
Columbia, South Carolina 29200

Secretary of State
Pierre, South Dakota 57501

Secretary of State
Nashville, Tennessee 37200

Secretary of State
Austin, Texas 78700

Secretary of State
Salt Lake City, Utah 84100

Secretary of State
Montpelier, Vermont 05601

State Corporation Commission
Richmond, Virginia 23200

Secretary of State
Olympia, Washington 98501

Secretary of State
Charleston, West Virginia 25300

Secretary of State
Madison, Wisconsin 53700

Secretary of State
Cheyenne, Wyoming 82001

Glossary of Legal Terms

Accommodation

An arrangement or engagement made as a favor to another, not upon a consideration received; something done to oblige, usually a loan of money or commercial paper; a friendly agreement or composition of differences.

Accommodation Note

One to which the accommodating party has put his name, without consideration, to accommodate some other party, who is to issue it and is expected to pay it.

Accommodation Party

One who has signed an instrument as maker, drawer, acceptor, or endorser without receiving value for it and for the purpose of lending his name to some other person as means of securing credit.

Acknowledgment

An acknowledgment is a public declaration or formal statement of a person executing an instrument made to the official authorized to take the acknowledgment, that the execution of the first instrument was his free act and deed. The written evidence of an acknowledgment, which states in substance that the person named herein was known to and appeared before him and acknowledged the instrument to be his act and deed. Generally substantial compliance with the form or requirements laid down in the state statute is essential to the validity of a certificate of acknowledgment. An acknowledgment to an instrument generally has three functions: (1) it may give validity to the instrument, (2) it may permit the instrument to be introduced in evidence without proof of execution, or (3) it may entitle the instrument to be recorded.

Agent

An agent is one who, by the authority of a principal undertakes to transact some business or manage some affairs on account of the principal, and to render an account of it. He is a substitute, or deputy, appointed by his principal primarily to bring about business relations between the principal and third persons.

Anticipatory Breach

In contract, a breach prior to a duty to perform, indicating an intention not to perform.

Articles of Incorporation

An instrument by which a private corporation is formed and organized under the general corporation laws.

Articles of Partnership

A written agreement by which the parties enter into a copartnership upon the terms and conditions stipulated in the contract.

Assignment

An assignment is a contract. It is a transfer or setting over of some right or interest in property, or of property itself, from one person to another.

Assignment for the Benefit of Creditors

The transfer by a debtor, without consideration, of part or all of his property to a party in trust to apply it to the payment of the debtor's indebtedness, with the surplus, if any, being returned to the debtor. It vests legal title in the assignee as trustee and places the property beyond the control of the assignor or the reach of his creditors, except as they have a right under the assignment to share in his estate.

Bank Draft

A check, draft, or other order for the payment of money, drawn by an authorized officer of a bank upon either his own bank or some other bank in which funds of his bank are deposited.

Bank Note

A promissory note issued by a bank or banker authorized to do so, payable to bearer on demand, and intended to circulate as money.

Blue Sky Laws

A popular name for acts providing for the regulation and supervision of investment companies, for the protection of the community from investing in fraudulent companies. A law intended to stop the sale of stock in fly-by-night concerns, visionary oil wells, distant gold mines, and other like fraudulent exploitations.

Board of Directors

The governing body of a private corporation.

Bond

In law, any written and sealed obligation, especially one requiring payment of a stipulated amount of money on or before a given date. A sum of money paid as bail or surety. One who acts as bail; bondsman.

Book Value of Stock

The net worth as shown by the books of the company; the net worth of all corporate assets less all liabilities, without allowing for the item of good will, unless it is shown clearly to be of certain value.

Breach of Contract

Failure, without legal excuse, to perform any promise which forms the whole or part of a contract.

Bulk Sales Acts

A class of statutes designed to prevent the defrauding of creditors by secret sale in bulk of all or substantially all of a merchant's stock of goods.

Bylaws

A rule or law of a corporation for its government which prescribes the rights and duties of the members with reference to the internal government of the corporation, the management of its affairs, and the rights and duties existing between the members.

Capital

That portion of the assets of a corporation, regardless of their source, which is utilized for the conduct of the corporate business and for the purpose of deriving gains and profits.

Capital Stock

The amount of money, property, or other means authorized by its charter and contributed, or agreed to be contributed, by the shareholders as the financial basis for the prosecution of the business of the corporation, such contribution being made either directly through stock subscription or indirectly through the declaration of stock dividends.

Cash Dividend

The distribution to shareholders of a portion of the profits or surplus assets of a corporation.

Cause of Action

The fact or facts which establish or give rise to a right of action, the existence of which affords a party a right to judicial relief. It is the right a party has to institute a judicial proceeding. A cause of action is that single group of facts which is claimed to have brought about an unlawful injury to the plaintiff and which entitles him to relief. In common parlance a cause of action is frequently referred to as an action, suit, cause, proceeding, case, lawsuit or a right "to sue the bastards."

Check

A commercial device intended for use as a temporary expedient for actual money, and generally designated for immediate payment and not for circulation.

Close Corporation

A corporation in which the majority of the stock is held by the officers and directors. For example, a corporation owned and operated primarily by a single family.

Closed Shop

A shop or business establishment where a worker must be a union member as a condition of employment.

Commerce

The exchange of goods, productions, or property of any kind. Intercourse by way of trade and traffic between different peoples or states and the citizens or inhabitants thereof, including not only the purchase, sale, and exchange of commodities, but also the instrumentalities and agencies by which it is promoted and the means and activities by which it is carried on, and the transportation of persons as well as of goods, both by land and by sea.

Internal commerce is that which is carried on between individuals within the same state, or between different parts of the same state.

Interstate commerce is that between states or nations entirely foreign to each other.

Intrastate commerce is that which is begun, carried on, and completed wholly within the limits of a single state, as contrasted with "interstate" commerce.

Commercial Paper

Bills of exchange, promissory notes, bank checks, and other negotiable instruments for the payment of money. Commercial paper is used to facilitate business transactions, as a substitute for the payment of money directly, and affords to the debtor an extension of time for the actual payment while offering certain protections and safeguards to all parties involved.

Common Stock

Corporation stock representing an interest that is subordinate to other interests in the corporation, such as bond and preferred stock, etc. Holders of common stock have an advantage over bondholders and preferred stockholders in that common stockholders are permitted to vote for directors, whereas preferred stockholders generally are not permitted to participate in corporation management.

Community Property

The property acquired by either spouse during marriage, other than by gift, devise, or descent based on the doctrine that property acquired during marriage belongs to the marital community. Community property states are Arizona, California, Idaho, Louisiana, Nevada, New Mexico, and Washington.

Contract

A promise, or set of promises, for the breach of which the law gives a remedy, or for the performance of which the law in some way recognizes a duty.

Corporation

An artificial person or legal entity created by or under the authority of the laws of a state or nation, composed, in some instances, of a single person and his successors, or another corporation, being the incumbents of a particular office, but ordinarily consisting of an association of individuals, who subsist as a body politic under a special denomination, which is regarded in law as having a personality and existence distinct from that of its members, and which is, by the same authority, vested with the capacity of continuous succession, irrespective of changes in the membership, either in perpetuity or for a limited term of years, and of acting as a unit or

104

single individual in matters relating to the common purpose of the association, within the scope of the powers and authorities conferred upon such bodies by law.

Doing Business

Within statutes on service of process on foreign corporations, equivalent to conducting or managing business. A foreign corporation is "doing business," making it amenable to process within a state, if it does business in the state in such a manner as to warrant the inference that it is present there—or that it has subjected itself to the jurisdiction and laws in which the service is made. The doing of business is the exercise in the state of some of the ordinary functions for which the corporation was organized. What constitutes doing business depends on the facts in each particular case.

Domestic Corporation

A corporation incorporated under the laws of a state, as opposed to a foreign corporation under the laws of another state or nation.

False Representation

A representation which is untrue, willfully made to deceive another to his injury.

Fiduciary

The term is derived from the Roman law, and, as a noun, means a person holding the character of a trustee, or the trust and confidence involved in it and the scrupulous good faith and candor which it requires. A person having a duty to act primarily for the benefit of another in matters connected with the undertaking. As an adjective it means something in the nature of a trust, having the characteristics of a trust, analogous to a trust, relating to or founded upon a trust or confidence.

Foreign Corporation

A corporation created by or under the authority of the laws of another state, government, or country.

Holder in Due Course

A holder who has taken a bill of exchange (check or note) complete and regular on the face of it, under the following conditions: (1) became holder of it before it was overdue, and without notice that it had been previously dishonored, if such was the fact; (2) took the bill in good faith and for valuable consideration, and that at the time it was negotiated to him he had no notice of any defect in the title of the person who negotiated it.

Holographic Will

A testamentary instrument entirely written, dated, and signed by the testator in his own handwriting. In some states, by statute, based on the Uniform Probate Code, it is only required that the signature and the material provisions of the will be in the testator's handwriting.

By requiring only the "material provisions" to be in the testator's handwriting, such holographic wills may be valid even though immaterial parts such as the date or introductory wording be printed or stamped. Under these statutes a valid holographic will might even be executed on some printed will forms if the printed portion could be eliminated and the handwritten portion could evidence the testator's will. For some persons unable to obtain legal assistance, the holographic will may be adequate.

Individual Retirement Account (I.R.A.)

The Pension Reform Act of 1974, Employee Retirement Income Security Act (ERISA), contained a provision which permitted a new type of tax-favored retirement program (I.R.A.) for employees and self-employed persons who are not covered by a tax-qualified plan, government plan, or tax-sheltered annuity arrangement. Most insurance companies and savings and loan associations have various programs for these plans.

106

Insolvency

The condition of a person who is insolvent, an inability to pay one's debts, having a lack of means to pay one's debts. One who is unable to pay debts as they fall due, or in the usual course of trade or business.

Legal Rate of Interest

A rate fixed by statute where it is not fixed by contract, and it is unless otherwise specifically provided the maximum rate which may be contracted for.

Limited Partnership

A partnership in which the liability of some members, but not all, is limited; such a partnership may be formed under most state statutes, which permit an individual to contribute a specific sum of money to the capital of the partnership and limit his liability for losses to that amount, upon the partnership complying with the requirements of the statutes.

Long Arm Statute

A statute allowing a court to obtain jurisdiction over a defendant located outside the normal jurisdiction of the court.

Majority Shareholders

Holders of more than 50 percent of the stock of a corporation.

Minority Shareholders

Holders of less than 50 percent of the stock of a corporation.

Minutes

Memoranda or notes of a transaction or proceeding. Thus, the record of the proceedings at a meeting of directors of corporations or shareholders is called "minutes."

Monopolies, Restraints of Trade, and Unfair Trade Practices

During the latter part of the nineteenth century this country had great growth in its economic and industrial development. There was a vast accumulation of wealth in the hands of corporations and individuals, and an enormous development of corporate organizations with the facility for combining into "trusts." As a result competition was threatened, price control was feared, and individual initiative was dampened—the evils that flow from monopoly practices.

In July 1890, Congress passed the *Sherman Antitrust Act*, 15 U.S.C. 1-7, which declared illegal all contracts, combinations, or conspiracies in restraint of trade or commerce among the states or territories or with foreign nations, and outlawed combinations or conspiracies to monopolize interstate or foreign trade or commerce.

The *Clayton Act*, 15 U.S.C. 18, was enacted in 1914 to reach certain specified practices which had been held by the courts to be outside the ambit of the Sherman Act. The purpose was to prevent economic concentration in American economy by keeping a large number of small competitors in business.

The *Robinson-Patman Act*, 15 U.S.C. 13, enacted in 1936, had as its main purpose to strengthen the Clayton Act regarding price discrimination.

Many of the states also have enacted antitrust laws; they are sometimes called "little Sherman Acts."

No Par Stock

Stock which is issued by a corporation without nominal value.

Par Value

The amount shown due on the face of the stock certificate.

Partnership

A voluntary contract between two or more competent persons to place their money, effects, labor, and skill, or some of them, in lawful commerce or business, with the understanding that there shall be proportional sharing of the profits and losses between them. An association of two or more persons to carry on as coowners a business for profit.

Piercing the Corporate Veil

In cases involving fraud or unjust enrichment, where the court refuses to recognize a corporation as an entity separate from those responsible for corporate activity, holding the corporation's alter ego liable, the court is said to pierce the corporate veil.

Qualification

The process by which a foreign corporation signifies its presence in the state and by which it submits itself to the laws and conditions of admission to do business in the state as prescribed by the laws.

Quorum

A majority of the entire body; such a number of the members of a body as is competent to transact business in the absence of the other members. The idea of a quorum is that, when that required number of persons goes into a session as a body, such as directors of a corporation, the votes of a majority thereof are sufficient for binding action.

S.E.C.

Abbreviation for Securities and Exchange Commission.

Share of Stock

The right which an owner has in the management, profits and ultimate assets of the corporation.

Shareholder

A person owning some part of the stock of a corporation.

Sub Chapter S Corporation

A corporation that is permitted to make an election to be taxed as a partnership, under Sub Chapter S of the Internal Revenue Code, thereby limiting individual shareholders' liabilities. Individual income is taxed, but the corporation is not taxed as a corporation.

Usury

An illegal contract for a loan or forbearance of money, goods, or things in action, by which illegal interest is reserved, or agreed to be reserved or taken. An unconscionable and exorbitant rate or amount of interest.

Will

An instrument executed by a competent person in the manner prescribed by statute, whereby the person makes a disposition of his property to take effect on and after his death.

A FREE ISSUE OF THE *CITIZEN'S LAW ADVISOR* IS WAITING FOR YOU!

Dear Friend,

Although this is the end of the book, it's just the beginning for you!

The *CITIZEN'S LAW ADVISOR* is a quarterly newspaper packed with human interest stories, advice on how readers are using the *CITIZEN'S LAW LIBRARY,* insights into tax shelters and other income sheltering and producing items, plus a complete book review and bookshelf section listing other titles in the field of layperson's law published by Prentice-Hall, Inc.

To receive your free complimentary issue of the *CITIZEN'S LAW ADVISOR* simply write your name and address on the coupon below and mail the coupon without further delay. Or call, toll-free, 1-800-228-2054 and tell the operator where you saw this announcement.

I look forward to hearing from you!

Sincerely yours,

J. Stephen Lanning

J. Stephen Lanning
Executive Vice President
Citizen's Law Library

CITIZENS LAW LIBRARY, Box 1745, 7 South Wirt Street, Leesburg, Va. 22075

Yes, please send me a free complimentary copy of the latest issue of THE CITIZENS LAW ADVISOR.

Signature _____

Name _____

Address _____

City _____ State _____ Zip _____

FYOC